THE MUSASHI
FIELD MANUAL

THE SWORD SAINT'S SECRETS FOR WINNING THE TESTS OF LIFE

Stickman Publications, Inc.
Seattle WA 98126

www.stickmanpublications.com

ISBN-13: 978-0-578-91380-3

Disclaimer:

THE MUSASHI
FIELD MANUAL

THE SWORD SAINT'S SECRETS FOR WINNING THE TESTS OF LIFE

MIYAMOTO MUSASHI
KRIS WILDER &
LAWRENCE A. KANE

STICKMAN PUBLICATIONS

Contents

Foreword by Iain Abernethy   vii

Introduction   xi

1. Accept everything just the way it is   1

2. Do not seek pleasure for its own sake   17

3. Do not under any circumstances depend on a partial feeling   27

4. Think lightly of yourself and deeply of the world   41

5. Be detached from desire your whole life long   59

6. Do not regret what you have done   73

7. Never be jealous   91

8. Never let yourself be saddened by separation   103

9. Resentment and complaint are appropriate neither for oneself nor others   113

10. Do not let yourself be guided by the feelings of lust or love   121

11. Have no preferences in all things   133

12. Be indifferent to where you live   149

13. Do not pursue the taste of good food   161

14. Do not hold onto what you no longer need   171

15. Do not act following customary beliefs   181

16. Do not collect weapons or practice with weapons beyond what is useful   205

17. Do not fear death   219

18. Do not seek to possess either goods or fiefs for your old age   243

19. Respect Buddha and the gods without counting on their help   255

20. You may abandon your own body but you must preserve your honor   267

21. Never stray from the way   287

Conclusion   301

About the Authors   307

Foreword

by Iain Abernethy

Portrait of Miyamoto Musashi (self-portrait) early 17th century (Edo period)

Miyamoto Musashi (1584 – 1645) is arguably one of the greatest warriors to ever to live. Undefeated in over sixty duels, his skill as a swordman is unparalleled. I think it would be fair to say that most martial artists who have been training for more than a few years have a copy of Musashi's *Go Rin No Sho* (*The Book of Five Rings*) on their bookshelf; some have even read it! This guide to Musashi's combative strategy is probably only second in modern day popularity to Sun Tzu's *The Art of War*.

While *The Art of War* focuses on the strategy employed by armies in large conflicts, *The Book of Five Rings* focuses on one-on-one altercations, hence its popularity with martial artists. *The Book of Five Rings* has also found much popularity in the business world. One can't help but wonder, however, what Musashi may have thought of that, what with merchants being the lowest class in samurai society on account of the fact they didn't produce anything, but simply distributed the result of the labour of others.

What is probably less well known is Musashi's *Dokkodo* (*The Way of Walking Alone*; sometimes translated as *The Path Alone*), which is essentially a brief summation of his philosophy of life. However, that too should be part of the study of all serious martial artists. Indeed, it is an interesting work for people who want to excel in any field.

Even those who don't know of Musashi have still experienced his cultural influence. As an example, the iconic catching of flies with chopsticks in the movie *The Karate Kid* is said to be based on tales of Musashi. In my case, the first time I came across Musashi was listening to the Iron Maiden song "Sun and Steel" on their 1983 album *Piece of Mind*. I had recently started karate training and the song inspired me to find out more about this legendary warrior. I have read *The Book of Five Rings* countless times since. On every reading, I realise there are ever deeper levels to the book and Musashi's repeated advice to "think about this deeply" is good counsel indeed.

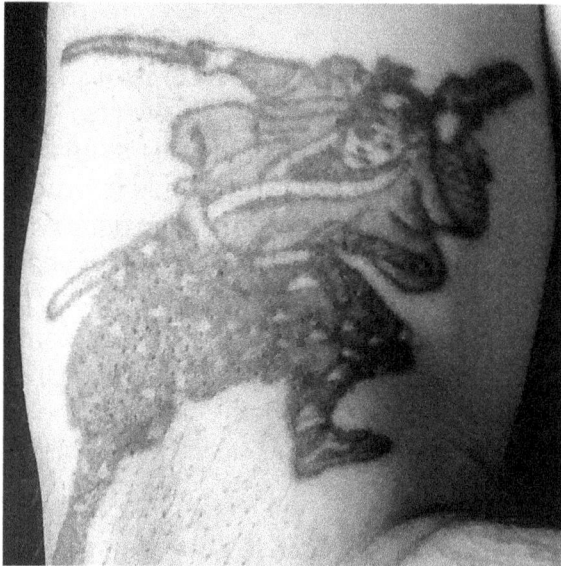

Iain's tattoo, faded after 27 years of commitment to the way.

When I turned eighteen, I decided to learn how to use the *katana* (samurai longsword) in order to better understand Musashi's advice. I studied that art for around five years. When I turned twenty-three, I got my first ever tattoo. I'm now covered in the things, but it seemed obvious way back then that my first tattoo should be of Musashi, and it should be placed on my right arm, my sword arm. I got a version of the iconic woodblock print of Musashi which was created by Japanese artist Utagawa Kuniyoshi (1798 – 1861). The passing of twenty-seven years has faded the tattoo, and it no longer looks as vibrant as it once did, but it's still there and worn with pride.

Both the *Book of Five Rings* and *The Way of Walking Alone* were passed onto Musashi's student Terao Magonojō (1611 – 1672) a few days before Miyamoto Musashi's death on the 13th of June 1645. They are incredibly important works.

The Way of Walking Alone is a fascinating read that contains much good advice from a man who certainly left his mark on the world and excelled in his field. While there is much we can learn from Musashi, a word of caution is also in order. We all have a propensity to see only the best in those we admire, yet Musashi was complex figure. For example, he seems to have placed little value on human relationships and is known to have killed a twelve-year old boy by ambush. In short, Musashi having defeated his older brothers, the twelve-year-old Matasichiro Yoshioka (1592 – 1604) challenged him to a duel to the death in order to restore his family's honour. Musashi ambushed him, killed the boy, and then fought off his retainers to escape.

To our modern sensibilities, the killing of a child in this way is not something that sits well with us to say the least. However, the truth is the truth no matter who utters it, and there can be no doubt Musashi has lots of interesting and insightful things to say. For example, his quote, "The ultimate aim of martial arts is not having to use them" is one that most would wholeheartedly concur with, even if Musashi himself didn't always follow his own advice.

Musashi's thinking also expands beyond combat. His insight can be applied to many things. As Musashi himself wrote, "If you know the way broadly, you will see it in everything."

Kris and Lawrence great friends, great men, and great martial artists. It is therefore a delight to write this modest foreword for this excellent book. Their reading of the *Dokkodo* makes the work accessible and applicable to our modern lives. You've made a smart move in getting this book. Don't let it collect dust on your bookshelf, put it into action!

....

Iain Abernethy has been involved in the martial arts since childhood. He holds the rank of 7th *Dan* black belt with the British Combat Association (one of the world's leading groups for close-quarter combat, self-protection and practical martial arts), the British Combat Karate Association, and the English Karate Federation. One of the leading exponents of applied karate, Iain has written a number of critically acclaimed books on the practical application of traditional martial arts and is well known for his work on the pragmatic use of the techniques and concepts recorded in traditional *kata* (forms). Iain's seminars, books, DVDs and articles have proven very popular with those groups and individuals who wish to practise their arts as the pragmatic systems they were originally intended to be. You can find out more on his website at https://www.iainabernethy.co.uk/.

There is nothing outside
of yourself that can
ever enable you to get
better, stronger, richer,
quicker, or smarter.
Everything is within.

Miyamoto Musashi

Introduction

Born in 1584, Miyamoto Musashi (1584 – 1645) grew up during the bloody Azuchi-Momoyama Period of feudal Japan with aspirations of becoming the greatest swordsmen of all time. He slew his first opponent in a duel at the age of thirteen and is known to have killed more than sixty highly-trained samurai (warrior, literally "those who serve") in single combat along with countless more on the battlefield. Thriving at a time when violent conflict was common and even a minor injury could lead to infection and death was a near miraculous feat of strategy, swordsmanship, and singlemindedness.

Nicknamed kensei, or "Sword Saint," for his unmatched prowess in battle, Musashi founded the unconventional Hyōhō Niten Ichi-Ryu style of swordsmanship, which directly translates as "Two Heavens as One," or more simply as "Two-Sword Style." Like most members of the samurai class, he was proficient in all aspects of warfare, yet he was skilled in the peaceful arts as well, an exceptional poet, calligrapher, sculptor, and artist.

Two years before he died, Musashi retired to a life of seclusion in a cave where he codified his winning strategy in Go Rin No Sho, which means "The Book of Five Rings." In preparation for his impending death in 1645, he both gave away his possessions and wrote down his final thoughts about life in a treatise he called Dokkodo, which translates as "The Way of Walking Alone." This volume was bestowed upon his favorite student Terao Magonojō (1611 – 1672), to whom Go Rin No Sho had also been dedicated.

Dokkodo is a short essay that contains a mere 21 passages, yet it is just as profound if not more so as Musashi's longer dissertation. His goal was to set his treasured student up for success, passing along his hard-earned wisdom about what makes a worthy and worthwhile life. The challenge, however, is that its very brevity leaves this writing open to interpretation, something that may have been tricky to decipher back when it was originally penned and has certainly become more difficult to comprehend today, more than three centuries after it was written.

You see, in a "Tab-A fits Slot-B" world, most of us are used to being told what to do rather than striving to figure things out for ourselves. That makes introspective analysis valuable in a multitude of ways, especially when we have an effective roadmap to guide our studies. That's where The Musashi Field Manual comes into play. It helps us discern our personal interpretation of Musashi's Dokkodo and in doing so grow wiser and more insightful from the process.

This is a structured yet open-ended workbook, designed to make you think. Every chapter begins with a precept from Musashi's Dokkodo along with some commentary related to the topic. It then provides a list of questions for you to contemplate. There are no standard responses, no answer keys to compare your findings against. It is incumbent upon you to discover your own unique, individual answers through self-examination, contemplation, and study. Musashi blazed the trail, now you have the privilege of following in his footsteps. Along the way you will discover new insights, and in doing so make your interpretation of his precepts uniquely your own.

Like most worthwhile endeavors, this workbook's value is directly correlated with the effort you put into it. Take your time. Think deeply. With thoughtful consideration and diligent study, you will be able savor the results of your hard work for the rest of your lifetime.

Enjoy!

The strong do what
they have to do, and
the weak accept what
they have to accept.

Thucydides

1.

Accept everything just the way it is

At first pass, this statement might appear passive, yet in practical reality it is not passive at all. In fact, it is an acknowledgement of the world, the way the universe behaves. It is recognition of how nature acts. In other words, it is not telling us to meekly accept whatever comes our way but rather warns us that we should be careful about our focus, wary of the filters through which we choose to observe everything that is around us. To discern what is real and perceive what is contrived.

Musashi is telling us to lean into and accept a clear vision of reality rather than an imaginative construct of our choosing. A constructive vision is akin to a stained-glass window. We know that we are observing sunlight coming through the opening, yet the colors are transformed and enhanced by the glass. As beautiful as it is, the window is still a human contrivance. The window's shapes and colors filter natural sunlight, changing its authentic hues. The thicker and more colorful the window, the bigger the alteration.

It is critical that we become aware of our filters while simultaneously not having too big of a filter left in place when we're done. Musashi and his students needed to know this cold. It was imperative for their survival in a world where highly skilled warriors regularly swung three-foot razor blades at each other on battlefields and in duels. Delusions cannot survive the theater of war. That was a serious state of affairs, one in which all samurai needed to see things for exactly what they were.

Although most of us will not regularly face life-and-death situations, we must heed this advice nonetheless. It is no mistake that Musashi placed this admonishment as his first precept. In fact, we believe these principles were written in order of importance. They are significant, all 21 of them, yet this one in particular is crucial. If we stubbornly continue view the world through the lens of our own delusion, we cannot implement this or any other of the Sword Saint's precepts.

The Dunning-Kruger effect, codified in 1999 by Cornell University psychologists David Dunning (1961 –) and Justin Kruger (1972 –), is a cognitive bias in which people wrongly overestimate their knowledge or abilities. This tends to occur because of a lack of self-awareness which prevents us from accurately assessing our skills. It can be challenging to work past this bias, yet whenever we question our understanding and conclusions rather than blindly accepting them, we find ourselves on the right path. Even in areas where we are 100% confident, we must acknowledge the possibility that there is something more to learn that we do not already know.

This is Musashi's challenge: we need to make every effort to see and acknowledge the way things are regardless of whether or not they are what we wish them to be. As you go through this workbook, you will undoubtedly find this first section tough. It is going to require meaningful introspection; all these things do. But then again, you knew that going in...

Check your biases. Be your own "devil's advocate," completely honest with yourself. It may be uncomfortable, but you will be far better off for the experience as this first precept lays the foundation for the rest of your journey.

How is my ego stopping me from moving forward
to the knowledge I need for a better life?

Can I name a specific example of letting my ego get in the way?

Was this example a one-off incident or part of a larger behavior?
Have I repeated it over multiple times?

When I look at my life do I measure it in a true
manner or am I clouding my own vision?

Of all of the things in my life which items do I truly have control?
Can I list 1, 2 or 3?

1

2

3

Change is inevitable; am I embracing the change with the flow?

Can I list a moment recently when I used flow successfully?

For what have I sold my piece of mind and
was it worth the price of the sale?

How can my current circumstance be exactly what I need, and even change my mind to appreciating what is happening?

What is an item in my life that appears to be one
thing that could be viewed in a new angle?

Can I accept the hand that is being dealt me?

Can I make the most of today and by extension
my life, today, now, and moving forward?

What is on the thing I can do today that moves me
closer to my goal, no matter how small?

Conclusion

What I am trying to do is illuminate the situations where accepting things as they are that have caused anxiety, stress or conflict. Now I have identified the areas of my life over which I have control and by extension those areas I have no control over. What is the one sentence I will write that expresses my new understanding?

....

....

....

....

When I focus on things beyond my control it creates

....

in my mind and it makes my body feel.

....

These feelings are emotions and are contrary to my being

....

and

....

so I can see the world clearly.

Work is the meat of life,
pleasure the dessert.

B. C. Forbes

2.

Do not seek PLEASURE for its own sake

Around 1500 BC the cult of Dionysus took hold. Dionysus (also known as Bacchus or Liber Pater) was associated with fruitfulness and vegetation, especially known as a god of wine and ecstasy. His cult was all about grapes, the wine, the harvest, all those things associated with drunken revelry, including dancing, singing, wild orgies, and animal sacrifices. While under their deity's inspiration, worshipers believed they possessed occult powers such as the ability to charm snakes, as well as preternatural strength that enabled them to tear living animal sacrifices to pieces before consuming them in ritual feasts called Dionysia (or Bacchanalia).

By modern standards the Dionysian cult seems a bit extreme, but hedonism was really not that uncommon historically despite the fact that such things were near universally frowned upon by societies of the time. Even today, the pursuit of pleasure for pleasure's sake has a negative connotation. Western literature is replete with examples and warnings against debauchery and shameless self-indulgence. Frequently these parables end with the pleasure-seeker achieving his or her sought reward only to find it bitter, proof that their lifestyle was not of any true or redeeming value.

We can find such warnings everywhere; it is the villain who is at the heart of such stories even though they may fancy themselves the hero. This pursuit of pleasure may not be the worst pursuit one might envision, yet we all know that pleasure found is found fleeting. It is akin to trying to capture smoke and pour it into a bottomless bucket. If all we care about is pleasure, we can never satisfy our desires.

Musashi was not alone in this admonishment. Luminaries across the ages have warned about self-gratification, railed against seeking pleasure for pleasure's sake. A few famous examples:

> "Whoever lives looking for pleasure only, his senses uncontrolled, immoderate in his enjoyments, idle and weak, the temper will certainly overcome him, as the wind blows down a weak tree."
>
> — **Gautama Buddha** (563 BC – 483 BC)

> "It is a sin to pursue pleasure as a good and to avoid pain as an evil."
>
> — **Marcus Aurelius** (121 – 180)

> "Forbidden pleasures are like poisoned bread; they may satisfy appetite for the moment, but there is death in them at the end."
>
> — **Tyron Edwards** (1809 – 1894)

> "There are seven sins in the world: wealth without work, pleasure without conscience, knowledge without character, commerce without morality, science without humanity, worship without sacrifice, and politics without principle."
>
> — **Mahatma Gandhi** (1869 – 1948)

As you to enter into this part of the workbook pay attention, special attention. Observe the substantial aspects of your life, consider your motivation, and examine how you treated those parts of your life with respect to pleasure.

The balance of life and work is the mark of a stable person.
Am I balanced between work and life?

The character that I seek for myself and the one I present
to the world — are they in alignment? How?

I have many strengths, some large some small.
Can I identify 3 strengths?

1 ....

....

....

....

....

....

2 ....

....

....

....

....

....

3 ....

....

....

....

....

....

How can I use those strengths?

What are the principles I have adopted, recently or long ago,
that steer me through the flow of change?

Pleasure is not a bad thing or experience, however seeking it for the sake of the experience can become a distortion. Pleasure can also be used to obfuscate an issue and understanding. Sometime I use pleasure as a replacement for

It is surprising to notice
that even from the
earliest age, man finds
the greatest satisfaction
in feeling independent.
The exalting feeling of
being sufficient to oneself
comes as a revelation.

Maria Montessori

3.

Do not under any CIRCUM STANCES depend on a partial feeling

The principle here is that feelings are okay, but we must make a distinction between feelings and partial feelings. Partial feelings are guesses or hunches; they are based on intuition rather than on known facts or scrutinized data. Partial feelings may ultimately prove to be right, but more often than not we find that they are incorrect, hence not to be acted upon without further information or exploration.

Think of partial feelings as concrete which can be set in place, but needs time to cure and harden to its full strength. Concrete often appears dry to the touch in as little as 48 hours, but in industrial settings it takes about 28 days, depending on the weather, for it to reach its full strength. Just as we cannot build a skyscraper on top of green concrete that has set but not fully cured and expect it to survive a windstorm or earthquake, we cannot make important decisions based on partial feelings.

The word "feeling" itself is interesting. In the English language, feelings can mean either internal perceptions or physical sensations. Feelings can be contrived. This contrivance is a convenient emotional sensation irrespective of its rationality. For example, the statement, "I feel like you're attacking me with your words," is pretty common. This declaration is an emotional expression of feeling. Sure, our feelings are real for us, but do they actually reflect the reality in which we find ourselves? Was the other person actually attacking, or merely expressing a logical disagreement that we were unprepared to hear?

Partial feelings in relationships such as this example can lead to preconceptions which are detrimental to and often undermine our rapport if not the entire relationship itself. They can make us listen for what we expect to hear rather than to understand what the other person actually meant or truly articulated. Consequently, if we have a partial feeling, we must pay attention. Scrutinize it. Examine the cues and clues that brought it to the forefront of our attention. But we must act like a detective, a real one not a television character, in so doing. We cannot act on a hunch alone, but must follow up, gather concrete information, and substantiate or disprove our gut feeling.

Hunches often stem from pattern recognition, meriting attention, but these partial feelings cannot be trusted without further examination. Keep this in mind as you navigate this section of the workbook.

What will happen if I peruse the items I have forestalled in life?

When I become angry, what would happen if I
waited some time before responding?

If I step back and watch, then test my observation, what would I find?

How can I test my own opinion before trusting it?

Despite the worst people can do or have done, can I
asses them, and their actions, emotionlessly?

Where have I put negative thoughts on top of
negative thoughts on top of my problems?

When important things do not go well, do I have a backup
plan? Do I have a way of extricating myself?

What emotions continually bring me to an errant conclusion?

Will the actions I take be based on cloudy or clear emotions?

Is disturbing news disturbing because of its true elements, or my reaction to the news?

Too much self-centered
attitude, you see, brings,
isolation. Result: loneliness,
fear, anger. The extreme
self-centered attitude is
the source of suffering.

Dalai Lama

4.

Think lightly of yourself and deeply of the WORLD

This fourth principle is a fascinating precept as it appears contradictory. History indicates that Musashi thought rather highly of his own accomplishments, making sure that everyone knew about them through his writings. There must have been plenty of brilliant strategists and exceptional tacticians in his day, yet most of their names have been lost to antiquity. We know of Musashi's exploits in large part because of the way he publicized them.

So, this dichotomy begs the question, how do we balance this principle with the rest of the Sword Saint's somewhat shameless self-promotion? The answer is found by understanding the context in which his precept was written. In this instance, the framework that provides meaning to Musashi's way of thinking was the caste system of feudal Japan.

In those days there was a four-tiered system for most of the population, with samurai (the hereditary warrior class, literally "those who serve") at the top followed by farmers, artisans, and merchants. Above the samurai were the nobility (technically also of samurai class) such as the emperor, shogun (chief military commander or military ruler), and daimyo (territorial lords, literally "large landholder"), along with various religious figures such as Shinto or Buddhist priests. There were also eta ("defiled ones") who lived below that caste system, beggars and people who performed distasteful work such as executioners, slaughterhouse workers, street sweepers, butchers, tanners, prostitutes, and undertakers too.

We can interpret what Musashi is saying here by considering that when we focus on the world and not ourselves, we are orient ourselves appropriately. This frames how we interact with those around us. In this fashion he understood his place within the hierarchy of his time, not in a derogatory way, but rather such that he clearly understood both his privileges and his responsibilities based on the societal norms with which he operated. This is the vital context, his implicit position within the feudal framework. From there he was able to balance his role with his time and space.

Think of it this way, if we needed to hire a surgeon to perform a life-saving operation we would not take comfort from a doctor who said, "Well, I'm the one-thousand and fifty-seventh best heart surgeon in this state." Clearly not, we would want somebody with the requisite knowledge, skills, and ability to do the job who both knows that they are the best and believes that they are the best.

In larger context still, the earth is about four billion years old. Humans, as a race, are about two million years old. So, according to current scientific understanding, the earth is far older than the humans who dwell upon it. This means that nature is huge while we are small. Earthquakes, tsunamis, plagues, and droughts are all part of nature. So too are breathtaking sunrises and gentle snows.

We can safely conclude that this precept is not about striving to become some sort of humble monk, walking around with our heads bowed low. No, not at all. This precept is about understanding our place, how we fit into the larger social construct as well as our place within nature and the universe itself.

As you begin this part of the workbook, you will find that the focus is on perspective and role. It is about how all of this meshes together. This analysis will illuminate how you see yourself within your strata as well as where you discover your place within different groups, organizations, relationships, and experiences.

What would my world look like if I took time before each decision?

Do I need to have an opinion about an issue or an action?
What would happen if I had no opinion?

What inconsequential comparison am I
allowing my mind to be clouded by?

What simple action can I take to dismiss these clouding thoughts?

What power do they take from me?

What is a good thing I can get from myself today
that moves me toward my goal(s)?

Seeking praise is hard work, and the results are
short-lived. Where in life you seek praise?

Are my opinions part of the problem?

How have my quick judgments caused me pain?

If I focus on something bigger than myself,
am I strong enough to not be lost?

How can I be the best I can be, just for this moment?
How can I do it in the next moment? How can I be
the best I can be one moment at a time?

Do I have envy over other people's abilities or can I focus inward, deepen and explore those things at which I am truly good?

Gain deep insight into your sense of self by taking
the PsychCentral Narcissistic Personality Quiz.
Completing the quiz takes about five minutes.

https://psychcentral.com/quizzes/narcissistic-personality-quiz/

Human behavior flows from three main sources: desire, emotion, and knowledge.

Plato

5.

Be detached from DESIRE your whole LIFE long

Desire is a driver. It has influenced men and women's behavior since before recorded time. You may be familiar with the story of Helen of Troy, who was reportedly the most beautiful woman in the ancient world. When she was kidnapped, war broke out over her retrieval. We can read about the 10-year Trojan War in the epic poem, the "Iliad" written by the Greek poet Homer (800 BC – 701 BC). Similarly, Romeo and Juliet, one of the greatest pieces of literature written by William Shakespeare (1564 – 1616) ended tragically. Here we have examples of war and suicide, both stemming from desire.

We can think of desire is a feral dog on a leash. Remove the leash and that dog runs wild. It runs into the neighbor's yard. The dog of desire gets into the trash, ripping things open, spilling and spreading it all around. It kills cats and squirrels, chases cars, bites the mailman, and humps the neighbor lady's leg. In other words, the dog of desire creates havoc.

Detachment, on the other hand, is about not possessing that dog. There is no leash, there is no dog. There is not even anything... In this fashion we may truly live in the moment, an admirable trait for a warrior whose every breath might easily be his or her last, yet meritorious for anyone to aspire to. In this state, desire can be set aside along with fear, hopelessness, and regret.

You see, small desires and large desires are all desire nonetheless. Some can be contained like small campfires within a ring of rocks, while others left unchecked become firestorms that consume everything in their path. Extinguishing a forest fire, even a figurative one, can be daunting, so the suggestion as you enter into this section of the workbook is to begin small. Start with minor things that might be found, managed, or eradicated relatively easily. Target your small fires, those that are easily extinguished.

Easy wins build a process for achieving victory that, in turn, leads to more and more success. Habitualized, this creates an upward spiral. As a result, difficult challenges appear ever more manageable. This is not a new formula, of course, yet it is good to restate here because it works so well. This continuous improvement methodology, leveraging small wins to produce larger ones, should be your mindset as you complete through this section of the workbook.

If I believe that I have no options,
what is the result and how should I act?

What or which of my desires is making life harder for me?

What can I stop desiring? How hard would it be?

What can I recognize as out of my control
and can I stop trying to control it?

What is the real cause of my attempt to imitate?
Is that imitation helpful?

If I stopped wanting would I truly lose any power?

I may not wish to be ruled by purpose, but rather by reason.
Can I identify where I lose my purpose and my reason?

If anger is not changing things, why do I indulge in anger?

How many times has anger done more harm
than the event that released the anger?

What irrational emotion or reaction needs to be snuffed out right now?

Has this world been so
kind to you that you should
leave with regret? There
are better things ahead
than any we leave behind.

C. S. Lewis

6.

Do not regret
what you have
DONE

This precept addresses a huge issue for many people today. Culturally, guilt is a deep motivator. Most of us carry it to some degree or another and it creates a negative weight on our psyche if not on our soul. What Musashi is saying here is that we should act like an NFL quarterback who just threw an interception during the first quarter of a playoff game; losers keep replaying that error in their head whereas winners flush that moment and move on. In other words, we must strive to learn from the past, plan for the future, but live in the now.

Remembering the past and learning from one's deeds is fine. Regrets can be part of the healing process. They can help us grow. But, lamenting past actions, dwelling in the past, was an absolute non-starter in Musashi's world. It should be that way in ours too. After all, we cannot change the past no matter how much whatever we may have done troubles us.

One of the regrets that many of us carry around is typified by a conversation that adult children often have with their parents. The parent expresses remorse about what he or she may have done, or should have done, while parenting. The child often returns with a comment like, "Children don't come with an owner's manual, so how could you have known?"

The challenge in this scenario is that there were books on parenting then, just as there are books on that subject now. Sure, the art and science of childrearing progresses over time, but there have always been resources available for those who sought them out. Courses, counseling, and coaching, all the necessary tools are out there somewhere, so the real issue is one of finding and applying them. Whatever our failing, it could have been moderated if not outright prevented had we properly prepared ourselves for the challenge ahead of time, a principle that should be applied to future endeavors but which cannot change the past.

Look back at the Azuchi-Momoyama Period of feudal Japan. It was a horrifically violent time where political unification was fashioned at the point of a sword, yet Musashi and others of his ilk lived by a moral code which helped them navigate that chaos. Their code assured that they knew their place in society and were able to discern right from wrong. That means that Musashi was in no way suggesting with this precept that we should laughingly walk away from our transgressions like a sociopath, but rather that we should not become mired in the past to our detriment. In other words, we should live and learn, ever moving forward without regrets holding us back.

We should all strive to make the best possible choices with the information we have at the time of each decision we make. The more important the decision, the more thought and analysis that should go into making it as we pointed out with the parenting example. This policy of doing what we know to be correct, of choosing wisely, avoids the tendency of creating regrets in the first place. Consider this as you progress through this section of the workbook.

As I look at the flow of life what lessons can be found in my actions?

Do I have the ability to be flexible? Maybe even change my mind?

Can I listen and hear the underlying message of what is being said?

If I can hear the underlying message, can I be adaptable enough
to change my mind when advantageous or necessary?

Where have I failed to see the bigger picture
and focused on the small and transient?

How can I listen and hear the underlying message of what is being said?

Am I centered and well-focused on the task at hand with a strong mind?

How many times have I placed limitations on myself
that are the tyranny of the mind and are unreasonable?

Work

Relationships

What would my world look like if
I focused completely on the moment, the now?

Worry over the past is pointless.
How often do I visit with the past and emotionally wallow?

Am I ready to lead where I am able?
If I am not ready, what is my reason, or worse, my excuse?

Am I truly willing to follow when appropriate?
If I am not ready to lead or follow what is my excuse?

If I am not the calm one in a situation
what can I do to become that person?

What do the acts of calmness feel like internally?

What do the acts of calmness look like externally, to others?

What would my world look like
if I focus entirely on the present moment?

Jealousy ... is a
mental cancer.

B. C. Forbes

7.

Never Be JEALOUS

Jealously is often about lust, love, or envy. We covet what others have and we do not, hence the idiom, "Keeping up with the Joneses." This expression refers to comparing ourselves with our neighbors as a benchmark of relative status. Typically, this is through the accumulation of material goods like cars, boats, or recreational vehicles, but it might also refer to the physical attractiveness of our spouse or significant other. In other words, failure to keep up with the Joneses implies socio-economic or cultural inferiority.

Jealously is a lot like a gateway drug. It is not a stand-alone emotion, but rather a pathway, a road to several other emotions. For example, jealously may lead to feelings of anger, loathing, or depression, and ultimately manifest in violence. Insecurity and helplessness can also stem from the root emotion of jealousy. It has also been linked to low self-esteem, increased stress hormones in the body, and a higher risk of Alzheimer's disease in women.

Those of us who are jealous perceive some lack deep within ourselves. We have a myopic, externally-based focus with which we compare ourselves against some measure which we have not yet reached or, in some cases, cannot ever attain. Extrinsic motivation refers to taking action not for its own inherent gratification or challenge, but rather for a separable outcome such as receiving rewards or avoiding punishment. Consequently, extrinsically motivated individuals can easily fall victim to other people's opinions, whipsawed by sentiments other than their own.

Musashi appears to have never engaged in jealously, at least not in what we can find in the historical record he left behind. We know for certain that he was intrinsically motivated, singularly-focused, and driven to succeed. He did what he wanted to, making decisions and taking actions because they furthered his cause. His unusual grooming habits, unconventional strategy, and unique two-sword style demonstrated that he had very little regard for what others thought of him despite living during a time when social customs and conventions held tremendous weight over most of the population.

Clearly Miyamoto Musashi was a singular individual. He stayed focused on his goals, directed his energy toward self-advancement, knew how to let the past go, and never strayed from his path toward success. If Musashi had been succumbed to jealously, we may very well not know anything about him today. He could have been just another body on the battlefield, an unlamented death like thousands of his brethren. Or, he might have become a cautionary tale of bad behavior and poor choices.

As you work through the section of the workbook you must ruthlessly seek out jealously in your own life and put a (proverbial) sword through its belly. Your task is to obliterate your jealousy. Welcome to the challenge.

How am I jealous, even in the slightest?

What is the tone of my view of the world?

Have I listened to the correct internal conversations?

Do I audit my thoughts regularly?

What emotion(s) holds me prisoner?

1

2

3

Can I name an untrue decision I have made?

Am I acting virtuously or in another way?
Yes____ or No____?
If I am acting other than virtuously,
what is my reason for acting in this manner?

Is my choice rationalized?
Am I justifying my non-virtuous action through a dance of thought?

Sadness is but a wall
between two gardens.

Khalil Gibran

8.

Never let yourself
be saddened
by

separation

Never let yourself be saddened by separation. Sadness dulls the senses. It mutes the vibrant colors of the world, transforming everything into dull shades of gray. Unchecked, sadness becomes the dominant and pervasive emotional element of our lives. It can lead to obsession, depression, or despair, inhibiting our ability to function competently (or in some cases function at all).

We have all known people who were saddened by separation, it is perfectly normal, but only to a certain degree. Pervasive, overwhelming sadness is dysfunctional. People consumed with sadness mope. They become unpleasant, difficult to be around or interact with for any length of time. They are not able to manage their relationships, enjoy the world around them, or perform their jobs satisfactorily. In fact, they appear to have but one focus in life, the separation they have suffered, and it dominates everything else.

Sadness is real. Musashi did not call it a lie or an illusion. What he did state categorically, however, was that being sad as the result of being disconnected from something must be a non-starter. It is important to note that he was not specific about the cause of such separations. Sadness is sadness. A lost love, family, job, school, or home could all be included in his statement. At this all-encompassing level, Musashi's precept could be a hard caution to accept. After all, who wouldn't be saddened by the death of a child, breakup of a relationship, loss of a treasured possession, or some similarly significant type of forced separation?

Nevertheless, in Musashi's mind a warrior could not afford to indulge in sadness. Anyone who has served in the armed forces, or even watched a competently-written war flick like Saving Private Ryan or Lone Survivor, knows the prototypical story of loss in combat. Soldiers acknowledge their bereavement at the appropriate time but never lose sight of their mission. There is a moment of solemness, of sadness, but it is not dwelled upon while the assignment remains incomplete.

We know that the preceding paragraph was a simplistic overview that lacks nuance... We cannot hope to come close to doing the grieving process justice with these few short and likely insufficient words, but hopefully the concept remains clear. The bottom line is that sadness cannot interfere with our ability to function. If it does, we must root it out, even if that means seeking professional help because we cannot or will not do it ourselves.

As you approach this section be aware of where separation in your life is beginning to turn, or has turned, toward sadness. Then consider how you have dealt with it.

Do I guard my time? How?

Is my attention to sadness?

Yes ____ No ____

How can I defeat sadness before it defeats me?

Is the sadness I need to defeat inside me?

What do having what I have and desiring
what I desire each say about me?

Is my sense of separation clouding my opportunity?

What do I value most?

There are times in
life when, instead
of complaining, you
do something about
your complaints.

Rita Dove

9.

Resentment
and complaint
are appropriate
neither for
oneself
nor others

Let us address this precept in reverse order, starting with complaint and then moving on to resentment: If we hear somebody complaining, they may not realize it but they are giving us a window into their mind. We gain insight. It shows us what their weaknesses are. In other words, they are telling us what is going on in their head and pointing out exactly what has provoked them. If we were so inclined, this reveal has set them up for us to exploit their vulnerabilities in the future.

Conversely, if somebody else is attentive as we complain, we have given them this very same insight too. We are opening up our minds for potential adversaries to rummage about within. This does not mean that process improvement discussions on one's job or personal conversations about events in one's life are inappropriate. These things can be beneficial. The difference is that complaint is peevish, it is merely venting our spleen with no attempt at conclusion or resolution. If we are trying to solve a problem that is good. If we are merely whining that is bad.

Sadly, complaint often becomes a game of one-upmanship, of tally-keeping. My bad day was worse than your bad day sort of thing... yet such games are an investment in dysfunction, an accounting of nothing. They may make us feel good for a moment, but ultimately grumbling does nothing to resolve our problems or address our issues in any meaningful way. And we look foolish for engaging in such folly.

In fact, complaint often stems from resentment, generally considered a caustic admixture of disappointment, disgust, anger, and fear, which is why Musashi covers these two topics together here. Resentment leads to complaint, which in turn gives those around us insight into how to push our proverbial buttons and steer us around by our emotions. Clearly that is not a good dynamic in any way, hence something we must learn to overcome.

In the 1999 movie, *For the Love of The Game*, Kevin Costner (1955 –) portrayed a veteran pitcher at the end of his career who was trying to prove to himself and others that he still had what it takes to play baseball at the highest levels of the game. There is a pivotal scene in the film where he is standing on the mound but becomes distracted by the sounds of the stadium, the fans, the opposing team players, vendors, and the like, yet says to himself, "Clear the mechanism." Suddenly he hears nothing at all, hence becomes able to place all of his focus where it belongs. It was his way of removing distractions and refocusing his attention on what was important with no resentment and no complaint. This scene, while written for Hollywood, is a good example of Musashi's precept in practical application. Real athletes in real games act similarly; those who play at the highest levels are universally able to ignore the chaos and focus on what is meaningful.

Keep in mind that there are two aspects to this principle, the observational and the internal. Couching these two elements in that context, consider what you are discovering from others and what you are revealing of yourself through resentment and complaint. As you go through this section of the workbook, take into account Musashi's admonition and consider how you can better live in the moment, concentrating on what is important here and now while flushing what is irrelevant.

Do I get hurt by even the smallest things? Briefly explain why it hurts.

Does anger drive any part of my life?

What result came of the times I have complained
or harbored resentment? Name an instance.

If I stopped resenting and complaining what would my world look like?

Love begins with an image;
lust with a sensation.

Mason Cooley

10.

Do not let yourself be GUIDED by the feelings of LUST or LOVE

Love is a universal and biologically-based emotion, yet Musashi warns against letting ourselves be guided by feelings of lust or love. What gives? Well, to figure that out we must determine what these two concepts, lust and love, actually mean... For example, the ancient Greeks codified eight different forms of love, *eros* (romantic/passionate), *philia* (affectionate), *agape* (selfless/universal), *storge* (familial), *mania* (obsessive), *ludus* (playful), and *philautia* (self-love). Other cultures make similar categorizations including concepts of sexual desire or physical attraction, affection amongst friends, family bonds, love of a deity or pantheon, and so on.

Of these two, lust and love, lust is irrational and consuming. A person engaged in lust becomes lost in the emotion. In fact, there is often a complete sublimation of the person within the emotion, a loss of thought process, control, and direction. Everything is guided by this lust. Lust burns like a brush fire; it spreads swiftly and runs out of fuel quickly. The fire burns hot, runs wild, and consumes itself. That is a precarious place to live.

When Musashi says that we should not be guided by feelings of lust, that is an easy admonition to understand if somewhat harder to obey. On the other hand, when Musashi says we should not be guided by love that is much more difficult to comprehend. You see, we are taught that love is a good thing. It is something to be desired, admired even. We are also taught that in the absence of love, brutality arises. Brutality rushing in to fill the void where love is absent is a phenomenon that can be pointed to over and over again throughout history.

For example, if we fall out of love with another person, we often proceed into the act of "othering" them. Othering is a phenomenon in which certain individuals or groups are defined as not fitting in within the norms of our social group. It is an effect that influences how people perceive and treat those who are part of the "in-group" versus those who are considered part of the "out-group." Acrimonious divorces illustrate this notion effectively; the former spouse and those in their circle of family and friends suddenly see the estranged partner in a different light irrespective of whether such judgement is warranted by their actions in the breakup.

When othering is successful, those in the out-group are villainized, considered less, treated worse, shunned, or even violently assaulted. Virtually any behavior taken against that ostracized group or individual can be justified in the minds of the people who did the othering. An example of this from Musashi's time were the *burakumin* ("hamlet people"), untouchables who lived as outcasts below the four-tiered feudal caste system in feudal Japan.

Originally *burakumin* were simply impoverished individuals who begged for scraps or accepted lowly or taboo occupations, but during the Tokugawa shogunate (1603 – 1867) the *burakumin* were officially segregated into separate communities where they were not permitted to marry above their station or accept employment in non-*burakumin* occupations. Although officially reintegrated into society during the Meiji Restoration (1868 – 1912), *burakumin* communities still exist in Japan today where a record of this designation in one's family lineage carries social stigma.

This twofold section is both easy and difficult. It is easy to see how we should not be guided by lust. To not be guided by love, on the other hand, is a difficult edict. This requires reconciliation. We must understand how we experience love, when it can be beneficial, and under what conditions it may be a hindrance. Consider this as you build out this section of the workbook.

When have explosions of emotion served me well?

Can I list one real-world example in the past that if I had held my emotions in check, the results might have been better?

How can I adjust my life to meter such emotions of lust?
What action will temper my emotion?

What can I do to preserve my serenity and push drama out of my life?

When I make my choices am I willing to, not just accept,
but lean into the results whatever they may be?

How many states of being can I name
that are better than living in drama?

Which of these states is the best for me to experience?

What is the second best?

I don't have one movie
that is my favorite, I have
about 25-30 favorites.

Jeff Bridges

11.

In ALL things have NO preferences

Let us enter into this precept using the topic of food. Not all that long ago, humans ate according to the four seasons. Fresh foods were consumed whenever they could be obtained, but provisions could be preserved through dehydration, such as storing fish, meats, and fruit under the sun while they dried out, through curing with salt, by cooling in root cellars, freezing in snow or ice, pickling with vinegar or alcohol, canning, fermentation, or burial in alkaline mud, ash, or the like. Without modern technologies to ubiquitously preserve, store, or distribute foods, most people ate whatever was locally available seasonally in order to survive.

Harvest celebrations occurring in the autumn acknowledged the bounty of food and the ending of the annual phase of hard work that made it available for the populace. Afterward during winter, people subsisted mostly on the preserved food and hunting or fishing where possible. By early spring the quality and the variety of what was available was significantly diminished, often unappetizing but consumed nonetheless because there was no other choice. Musashi speaks from this time, when even though he was a member of the elite samurai class, he had far, far less choice in his food than we do today.

The same thing pertains to other aspects of our lives such as entertainment. It is not about what is given, but rather about what is available. We no longer have to wait for a traveling bard or circus to come through town for our recreational enjoyment. Exponential growth of media and proliferation of channels has changed viewing behaviors. The challenge is that with so many choices we often believe that we must be discerning, even at the risk of missing out on valuable experiences we never learn about.

In school we are often taught that there is only one right answer, one proper way to solve a problem or equation, yet in everyday life we come to realize that is rarely the case. There may be some answers that are better than others, some solutions that are more or less innovative than others, but there is usually more than one right choice. In fact, if we steadfastly hold to our preferences without examining other options, we are virtually guaranteed to miss out on the choice that best suits our needs. We are locked into the answer we know irrespective of whether or not it is right. Here are a few famous examples of this dynamic:

In 1889, American inventor Thomas Edison (1847 – 1931) said, "Fooling around with alternating current is just a waste of time. Nobody will use it, ever." Wrong! Today, nearly every household in the world is powered by alternating current which makes it possible for us to enjoy refrigerators, dishwashers, air conditioning, televisions, computers, and more.

In 1899 Charles H. Duell (1850 – 1920), Director of the US Patent Office, categorically stated, "Everything that can be invented has already been invented." Obviously, he was mistaken. Massively mistaken. He did not predict advances like antibiotics, motion pictures, cellphones, contact lenses, computers, the internet, and jet planes, to name a few.

In 1943, IBM's CEO Thomas Watson (1874 – 1956 said, "I think there is a world market for maybe five computers." A monumental miss! Not even close... He only underestimated that forecast by about 4.1 billion.

In 1946, 20th Century Fox studio executive Darryl F. Zanuck (1902 – 1979) boldly proclaimed, "Television will not be able to hold on to any market it captures after the first six months. People will soon get tired of staring at a plywood box every night." A bit of a blunder there; even though viewership has declined over the last decade, the average American still watches a bit more than four hours of television a day.

The illustrations of this point are legion so we will not belabor them. Some may take the precept of having no preferences as some form of austerity. It should not be seen that way, however. Austerity for austerity's sake is an affectation. Consider instead the idea of being open to new opportunities and experiences without being overly set in our ways.

It may not be possible to literally have no preferences, but the goal of making your preferences as small as possible is achievable. The more we remain open to possibilities in all aspects of our lives the more we can create opportunity. Keep this in mind as you fill out this section of the workbook.

Am I happy with my place in life? How am I
able to enjoy what life brings me?

Do I focus on other people's errors? How can I simply observe?

What methods can I use to separate
the important from the unimportant?

Are the methods I just listed emotionally or fact-based? Which of them serves me best?

Am I satisfied to have no effort of opinion about
things that don't matter in the larger picture of life?

Is it necessary to choose a side on every issue?
What would happen if I just let some things pass?

What kind of mental practice will bring me calmness and focus?
Be specific.

Of all of the things in the world, what do I truly own?

Can I roll with a punch life brings? How have I done this in the past?

This life has a role for me.
In what ways am I acknowledging it or fighting it?

Every day is a journey, and
the journey itself is home.

Matsuo Basho

12.

Be indifferent to where you LIVE

Although social mobility has been possible historically in certain societies, it has never been as easy as it is with modern technology today. For example, in the year 2020 there were approximately 46.8 million millionaires in the world, 67.7% of them self-made. By contrast, in feudal Japan the caste system was hereditary. If we were born into an artisan family, we became artisans as did our children and our children's children.

Only about ten percent of the population were born samurai during Musashi's day, and it was extraordinary unusual for someone of a lower class to be advanced to any higher rank let alone to that lofty status. That singular honor could only be bestowed by a member of the ruling nobility such as *daimyo* (territorial lords) or appropriated by force of arms which was nearly impossible for untrained peasants to do. Interestingly enough, historical records do show that four European *gaijin* (foreigners) gained samurai status, William Adams (1564 – 1620), whose exploits inspired James Clavell's Shogun, Eugene Collache (1847 – 1883), Jan Joosten van Lodensteijn (1556 – 1623), and Edward Schnell (1830 – 1911).

In terms of moving from place to place, we have far more options today than at any time in human history. For example, a $693 flight from New York to Singapore covers 9,540 miles in a bit less than 18 hours, a trip that would have been unaffordable for most, fraught with dangers, and have taken over a month-and-a-half to complete a century ago. Or if we do not want to fly, we could near instantly communicate from here to there via cellphone, audioconferencing, or video call. Technology makes the world a very small place.

In Musashi's time, however, most people were born, lived, and died within about a 25-mile radius. Sure, there were outliers such as nomads, traders, and herders, but travelers in those days were both brave and remarkable. You see, when a person left his or her home village their safe return was far from assured. These intrepid explorers brushed up against rival tribes, novel diseases, unforgiving seas, and a host of other challenges that most of us do not have to worry about now.

Although Musashi never left the islands, he travelled extensively throughout Japan in *musha shugyō* (warrior pilgrimage), honing his skills with duels as well as on the battlefield, fighting for a variety of warlords and causes. Although he never committed to a life of service to any particular daimyo, he fought often and relentlessly in order to advance his legend. One can imagine that it was relatively easy for a person who slept alongside a field one night, in a cave another, and perhaps at an inn or a castle yet another to be indifferent about where he lived.

Should we follow his example? This is an interesting attitude as it must be noted that for all his travels Musashi remained immersed in the same culture and station wherever he went. He did not have the option to travel to a foreign country just to see what it was like. He was born a samurai and died a samurai, so while he could move about based on the prospects of opportunities to advance his cause, he did not have the option to change jobs because something beyond swordsmanship sounded more interesting for him to try. That is a very different circumstance than most of us find ourselves in today.

Similar to the previous precept about having no preferences, it is important to be open-minded, yet our world and its choices differs significantly from Musashi's. Consider the raw utilitarianism of his words against which to measure and compare. In this fashion, you can determine how this precept matches up with your values and what you should do about it.

Which of my desires are real?

Have I built a self that is internally strong?

What are the things in life that are real?

In what ways can I live a healthy life no matter
the atmosphere, the setting?

What causes of distress can I tune out, eliminate from my life?

What can I learn from the place I am living in right now?

It's easy to impress me. I don't need a fancy party to be happy. Just good friends, good food, and good laughs. I'm happy. I'm satisfied. I'm content.

Maria Sharapova

13.

Do not pursue the taste of good food

We can see an interesting corollary between many of Musashi's precepts and the "Seven Deadly Sins" of Christian tradition compiled by Saint Gregory the Great (540 - 604), the Bishop of Rome who founded the medieval papacy. These sins include Lust (addressed by Musashi in precept 10), Gluttony (related to pursuit of good food here in precept 13), Greed, Sloth, Wrath, Envy (addressed by Musashi in precept 7), and Pride. While they do not completely align, we can certainly see a cross-cultural validation for many of his ideas.

This 13th precept could be interpreted as an admonition against eating good tasting food, warning us away from the salty, the fat, and the sweet, but that view is incorrect. The operative word here is, "pursue." Musashi is telling us to not attempt to capture the taste, nor employ extraordinary measures to gain flavorsome food, as opposed to consuming whatever is available to meet our nutritional needs. In his view, it was not a valuable use of his time as well as a wasted emotional investment. When considered in this light, it can be a useful admonition.

Today we face challenges that Musashi never foresaw, such as the impulse candy rack at the grocery store checkout counter. Such opulence was not predicted. Further, the marketing that near continuously assails us today is something he never would have imagined. The point here is that this precept is more valuable today in many ways than it was in Musashi's time, since we have far more options and temptations.

Pleasure leaves our bodies quickly. And in some cases, the fleeting pleasure can be damaging. For example, the euphoric effects of heroin consumption may leave the body, but the damage to a user's vascular system remains. A collapsing of the vascular system can leave a junky no choice but to inject into an open wound as an emergency room nurse once related to the authors.

Many people understand that what their dog or cat consumes directly ties to that pet's wellbeing, hence seek out veterinarian-sanctioned brands or blends, yet fail to draw a correlation between their own consumption habits and physical or mental health. Nevertheless, medical science proves that over-pursuit of good food has serious detrimental effects on a person's body. Even if we eat "clean," eating too many calories is problematic. Obesity is serious because it is directly linked with both poor mental health outcomes and reduced quality of life. It is also associated with diabetes, heart disease, stroke, and several types of cancer, the leading causes of death worldwide.

We can see Musashi's wisdom here. We may enjoy what presents itself with respect to good food, but must take caution to avoid excess. Overzealous effort expected in gaining access to the taste of good food can be both hazardous and undesirable. Consider this as you fill out this section of the workbook. Examine both what you eat along with when and why. Are you fueling your body nutritionally or merely pandering to your acquired tastes?

How would I feel if I diminished my own wants
when it comes to fine food and drinks?

If my tastes in food are simple, what would happen if I
extended that simplicity to other arenas of my life?

Are my desires countermanding my bigger goals?

Are you saying no to the wrong things and yes to the good choices?

What wants can I remove from my day?

If I removed a want this one day what would the results be?

Wealth consists not in
having great possessions,
but in having few wants.

Epictetus

14.

Do not hold
ONTO WHAT YOU
no longer
NEED

Musashi traveled light. He lived light, and it is a reasonable assumption although not well-documented historically, that he owned little beyond what he carried with him. In his last days he lived in a cave, presumably one that was not well-appointed, and gave away all of his worldly possessions shortly before his death.

This behavior was consistent with his way of life. Clearly, he was a man who did not hold on to possessions that he no longer believed he needed. This precept becomes more relatable, however, when broken down into two elements: utility and sentiment.

When viewed through the lens of utility, we must ask ourselves, "Can I use this?" "Does it help me meet my tactical or strategic goals?" That is a pretty straightforward analysis. If we have a collection of items we cannot use, or have not used for months or years, we can easily give them to friends or neighbors who may find them valuable, donate them to charity, sell them, or find some other appropriate way to dispose of them.

Sentiment, on the other hand, is more complex. It addresses emotional attachment. For example, Wilder owns a broken baseball bat. That bat serves no utilitarian purpose, it cannot be used to play the game. We might think that a broken-bat belongs in the garbage, but the fact that it was once owned by his uncle and used in a game sixty-five years ago changes the equation. Its value lies in the remembrance. Is that possession, the bat, useful? Not really, but Wilder keeps it anyway.

Here are two examples to help bring clarity to this precept. Wilder knew a retired priest who upon his death had whittled all of his worldly possessions (outside of his clothing) down to fit inside of a single box. This man had edited his whole world down to that one large box. On the other side of the equation, Wilder also knew of a woman who was such an extreme hoarder that she purchased the house adjacent to her residence so that she had a place to store more of her belongings.

Most folks are neither ascetics nor are they hoarders, but rather fall somewhere in between. The "right" number of possessions for any individual is a personal choice, based on utility and sentiment of what we have accumulated. Nevertheless, it is useful to make an assessment from time to time and evaluate where we stand. Many people use their annual spring cleaning for this purpose.

When working through this section, consider how long it has been since you have organized your closet, cleaned out your garage, or made an inventory of what's stored in your spare bedroom. Do you even remember everything that you own and know where it is located? Are you holding on to possessions that you no longer need?

Are the items, possessions I am pursuing actually worth it?

Do my wants match my life plan or are they at odds?

What truly treasured things do I sell or give away at a cut rate?

How am I creating energy for my good behaviors?

Am I willing and able to do the right things
even if there is no promise of rewards?

False friendships and bad influences are not in alignment with my life goal. Where are they damaging and what actions can I take to fix this?

Life is very, very simple
and easy to understand,
but we complicate it
with the beliefs and
ideas that we create.

Don Miguel Ruiz

15.

Do Not Act
FOLLOWING
Customary Beliefs

This principle seems at odds with the samurai code of ethics, *bushido*. *Bushido*, which translates as "way of the warrior," was a protocol that regulated the samurai's attitudes, behavior, and lifestyle through a variety of cultural and legal codes, practices, philosophies, and principles. Musashi's dress, weapons, and culture were all are quite customary, yet there were aspects of his behavior that were at odds with this samurai protocol. He had a tendency to ignore the rules when it suited his purposes.

For example, in 1600 he found himself on the losing side of the Battle of Sekigahara (which paved the way for the Tokugawa *shogunate*), hence became *ronin* (a masterless samurai, literally "wave man"), which was considered vagrant, disruptive, even rebellious at that time. Shamed by the loss, he could have committed *seppuku* (ritual suicide) as his adopted son Mikinosuke (1604 – 1626) later did when his liege-lord died, or petitioned a new *daimyo* (territorial lord) for patronage, but chose another path.

He was progressive in other ways too. For example, he kept a full head of hair when convention was to shave one's forehead. He rarely bathed because he felt it would leave him vulnerable to attack, despite living in a culture where cleanliness was expected. He also had a disrespectful set aside his steel *katana* for a wooden *bokken* sword, leverage psychological warfare to defeat his adversaries, switch sides when it suited his purposes, and fight with two weapons when convention was to use only one.

Acting in a contrary manner is not necessarily a means for success, nor is being contrarian merely for the sake of opposing the norm productive. Such behavior creates low trust within the community and taken to the extreme leads to shunning or banishment. So, although Musashi was somewhat selective in how and when he followed the rules of samurai life, he did not go so far as to break the trust of his compatriots. The men next to him in battle knew that he could be counted upon when steel met steel. In other words, he may not have been the guy we would have wanted to spend the night before a battle drinking with by the campfire, but when blades crossed there was no one better to have on our side to assure our ability to successfully complete our mission.

Perhaps a better way to translate this precept would be to say, "Think for yourself." Simply because something is normal or has been customary for a certain period of time does not necessarily mean that it still serves us well. Or that the custom is remains relevant or valuable…

Consider the case of Polaroid, the company whose name was once synonymous with picture-taking. In the 1960s and 70s Polaroid held a monopoly on instant photography while also owning about 20% of the film market and 15% of camera market worldwide. As a corporation they were a powerhouse, yet they failed to embrace emerging technologies and ultimately went bankrupt in 2001.

All enterprises go through a standard business cycle from launch through growth, shakeout, maturity, and decline. The good ones are able to regularly create new products or services or otherwise reinvent themselves and drive a lifecycle extension, but the ones who do not or cannot wind up like Polaroid. Since about a third of all companies go bankrupt in their first year, and half by their fifth, following the standard convention would appear to be a path to failure in business.

We need to regularly ask ourselves if the customs we follow still meet our goals. Are they working? Has something changed that should make us reevaluate our choice or our direction? As you work through this section, do a creative audit of where you stand. Then, as any skilled carpenter will do, measure twice and cut once.

Am I standing with what is true and correct or with the horde?

Recently I fell in with the horde when I

Here is a moment where I stood with what
was true and not with the horde

Where have I transferred my freedom for a comfort?

What small act can I take to get my freedom back?

Is my action good? How often do I use forethought?

In what was is my power to choose strong?

As change happens do I judge it as bad verses good?
Is this viewpoint destructive? In what ways do I see
the advantage of abandoning judgment?

Is my assessment of change realistic?

Is my assessment of change one of advantage or injury?

In what ways do I overly depend on others?

What actions can I take to make my own good luck, to be ready to take advantage when the opportunity appears? Name three.

1 ....
....
....
....
....

2 ....
....
....
....
....

3 ....
....
....
....
....

Can others see my principles or do I hide them?

Am I acting in accordance with my chosen path, today?

Yes   No

I am going to take this one action of ....

....

....

....

....

....

....

....

....

....

....

....

for the sole purpose of getting aligned with my principals.

Do my principles color my life or am I letting the world color my life?

Am I inspecting my first impressions or simply accepting without review?

What choices have I made recently where my
first impression was less than optimal?

How can I be more accepting of my conditions?

How can I be more willing to wait until the correct time?

How can I better identify the correct time to act?

With acceptance has my view of my surrounding situation changed?

How would I rate my self-confidence?
(circle the correct number 1=Lowest, 10=Highest)

Overall	1	2	3	4	5	6	7	8	9	10
At Home	1	2	3	4	5	6	7	8	9	10
At Work	1	2	3	4	5	6	7	8	9	10

Does this rating effect the way I see the world, and how?

There's never enough
time to do all the
nothing you want.

Bill Watterson

16.

Do Not Collect
Weapons Or
Practice With
WEAPONS
Beyond What Is
USEFUL

This precept is specific, its context directed toward battle and warfare. It would be ridiculous for an army to practice training with weapons they know that they are never going to use. Musashi elaborates on this topic in the *Go Rin No Sho,* where he writes about being familiar with other weapons so that we will understand their strengths and weaknesses, but not necessarily being adept with weapons we do not use.

Every warrior should become familiar with how the instruments of destruction they might face on the battlefield could be used against them, that's prudent. Nevertheless, we all know that it is not possible to master every conceivable weapon in one's arsenal which is why soldiers specialize. As for our primary weapon, that is what we must strive to master. The rest we should merely know about.

Former Head Coach of the Los Angeles Rams, Seattle Seahawks, and Buffalo Bills Chuck Knox (1932 – 2018) was one of the first NFL coaches to have his teams regularly practice the plays that they expected to use at the end of games when they desperately needed to score, something quite common today. Nicknamed "Ground Chuck," for his tendency to call running plays, he is quoted as saying, "Practice without improvement is meaningless." Musashi would undoubtedly have appreciated that sentiment.

Interestingly, Coach Knox was also known for practicing his cursive penmanship on a daily basis. Perhaps this was a mediative method, meaningful time away from intensity of his coaching job, but whatever his reason he set time aside for this practice. We do not know why he did it, but we do know that he found such practice useful. Likewise, we must assure that our time is used deliberately for whatever purpose we devote ourselves to. In other words, we must set aside any weapon, tool, phone app, or other instrument that wastes our time because it no longer suits our needs.

When auditing this divestment, it is useful to break the act up into three columns representing our mind, body, and spirit. Populate the columns to see what aspects are in need of edit. What should you set aside to assure that you are not collecting weapons that are no longer useful?

If what I am doing doesn't fit with my life plan and
I stopped doing it, what would happen?

Will this action affect only this single item, or will
it permeate other aspects of my life?

Do I have a habit of continuing a path because of the sunken cost fallacy? What is a recent example?

Am I doing a good job of reviewing my energy expenditures? What is a recent example?

Can I be like a cat, relaxed when it is time to relax
and intently alert when appropriate?

What do I do that feeds my mind?

What do I do that is less than rewarding? Is it worth my time?

Does my relaxation and entertainment feed me well or
is it mental junk food? What is a recent example?

What am I getting in return for my effort?

Professionally

Personally

In my relationship(s)

I spend my time freely, but at what cost to me?

Do any of my possessions that I think I own actually own me?

The proper function of man is to live, not to exist. I shall not waste my days in trying to prolong them. I shall use my time.

Jack London

17.

DO NOT
FEAR
DEATH

We all die, it is unavoidable. Musashi is not arguing about the inevitability of our impending demise, but rather saying, "It is coming, be ready." Clearly there is a huge spiritual and cultural element to this topic, as different societies view the specter of death differently.

In mythological lore, the Grim Reaper is the personification of death. He is typically represented as a hulking, black-cowled skeleton carrying a scythe. This symbology is important as the Grim Reaper can be seen as a terrifying apparition by some or as a release from a horrific existence by others. The scythe he carries was used for centuries before the invention of horse-drawn or motorized machinery to cut grains and grasses, an act which could be interpreted as killing the plant or as transforming it to a new use, in this instance wheat or barley to eat or, perhaps, thatch for a roof.

In Musashi's time, warriors believed that they must overcome any fear of death lest it impede their ability to serve their masters wholeheartedly. For example, in *Hagakure* (which translates as "Hidden by the Leaves"), written by Yamamoto Tsunetomo (1659 – 1719), there is a passage which reads, "The way of the samurai is found in death... This is the substance of the way of the samurai. If by setting one's heart right every morning and evening, one is able to live as though his body were already dead, he gains freedom in the way. His whole life will be without blame, and he will succeed in his calling."

Death was not something Musashi was indifferent to, he dealt with it and dealt it regularly, yet it is clear that he wants us to hold the inevitability of death in a different light than most folks do. He expects acknowledgment and acceptance. If we argued backward to the Grim Reaper, Musashi is telling us that the Grim Reaper is ever present and that we should consider the inevitability of meeting him and be prepared.

Somewhere around the age of ten children begin to realize that death is a universal, irreversible, and nonfunctional state. As we age, our attitudes about end of life tend to evolve, though about a quarter of the adult population reports that they have given no or very little thought to the subject whatsoever. Less still take any action. In fact, 68% of Americans do not even have a will, living trust, health care directive, estate plan, or durable power of attorney. Since death eventually comes for us all, it is a subject worthy of our consideration.

As you fill out this section, be aware of the place where you begin. What is your perspective about death? Is it one of fear, dread, acceptance, or welcoming? Take a moment and orient yourself before beginning, then roll up your sleeves and go to work.

Am I in control of my emotions, my anxieties, or do they possess me?

What actions do I take that disrupt my life, my
flow, costing me time and quality of life?

Is my mind a good monarch or ruthless dictator?

Specifically, where does my mind dictate a fear?

Am I flexible enough to allow what might happen? In what ways?

Can I take a blow and survive? In what ways?

When was a time when I took a blow and survived?
How did I do it? What did I learn??

Why did I fail? What did I learn?

Have I made the mental choice to move forward or retreat?

Where have I made this choice?

Do I fear for my life?

If I do fear for my life, is the fear the correct tool to use to protect my life? What could or should I do differently?

The immutable rule of life is it ends in death.
Am I living, or busy not dying?

What emotion or thought is a better tool to use to protect my life?

What acts can I take on to make living about living and not dying?

What can I do to live now while I still can?

How can I better prepare for the losses I fear?

Am I foolishly afraid of losing? What can I do about it?

What real-world difficulties am I solving with this new tack in life?

The present moment is all we have;
what behaviors am I taking on to live in the now?

Wealth consists not in
having great possessions,
but in having few wants.

Epictetus

18.

Do Not Seek to POSSESS Either Goods or Fiefs for Your Old AGE

Musashi never married, and while there are rumors that he may have fathered child with a courtesan named Kumoi, he had no known natural descendants. A *ronin* (masterless samurai), he was never granted lands or properties for his service to a *daimyo* (territorial lord). He did, however, want his legacy to endure beyond his lifetime so he adopted two sons, Mikinosuke (1604 – 1626) and Iroi (1612 – 1678). Mikinosuke committed ritual suicide after the death of his *daimyo* Honda Tadatoki (1596 – 1626), who succumbed to tuberculosis, whereas Iroi became the highest-ranking vassal of *daimyo* Ogasawara Tadazane (1596 – 1667) by the age of 26.

So, this begs the question, other than his reputation what did Musashi actually own? Not much by most accounts, but what he did possess he clearly valued and used. It is worth noting that living and fighting in close proximity to nobility, he no doubt observed their desire for possessions and power. However, we do not believe that he held these individuals in low regard despite never aspiring to become one of them.

Even though Musashi held himself apart to large degree, living in feudal times at the top of the hierarchy was substantially different than living at the bottom. Those who owned property and controlled their own resources had the best opportunity for survival. They had vassals to keep them safe, collect revenues, and carry out their will. They may not have had the best of everything, but they rarely lacked for sustenance, supplies, or medical care. In a caste system it was important to hold onto one's status or, when feasible, better one's position through earning favors, waging warfare, or any other means possible.

Musashi was a product of his self-constructed environment. As the caste system held people static in their social positions, the most effective path to ascending the hierarchical ladder was through violence. Those who were brave and mighty enough could take what they wanted and suppress any retaliatory actions against them from others.

In other words, the caste system required violence for social mobility and a better life. Sure, special dispensation could be granted by one's liege lord, but in most instances that was reward for an act of violence performed in the *daimyo's* service. Since Musashi had no family to care for nor property to defend, he could stand apart from this dynamic, at least to large degree. As extreme as this may appear in the context of those times, Musashi was unencumbered by the needs, wants, and desires of most of his brethren.

Since he was not shackled to the system, hence able to forge his own path, Musashi would certainly have been a proponent of others following a similar approach. He was born Buddhist, and although not particularly religious was influenced by Buddhist and Shinto philosophy, especially later in life. Afflicted by what was believed to have been thoracic cancer, he knew with certainty when his end drew near, and that likely colored his perspective on material possessions as well.

You have probably noticed that there is more speculation in this chapter than in those preceding it. Are we reading a lot into his precept? Certainly, without question... The idea is to stimulate your thinking and lead you to audit your value structure, its use, and purpose.

Possessions are only useful while you are alive, so the older you are the less you may feel a need for material wealth, save for what you would like to pass along to your heirs. Does this resonate or do you hold a different opinion? As you go through the workbook here, consider what you value and why.

We value nice and expensive things, but what are they really?

Is what I value a part of a larger goal or a status symbol?

Where have I found money to be more important than my own name?

Am I actually improving or speeding after the
ungraspable smoke of self-importance?

Is my ego easy to be around or is it imposing and dominating?

This life has tasks for me. Can I identify those tasks? List them here:

Once I have identified these life tasks can I,
will I, step forward to meet them? How?

God gave us the gift
of life; it is up to us
to give ourselves the
gift of living well.

Voltaire

19.

Respect Buddha and the GODS without Counting on Their Help

This is a powerful, yet unsurprising statement coming from a strong, self-made personality like Musashi. In feudal Japan the polytheistic Shinto religion was predominate. Shinto, which translates as, "the way of *kami*" (generally sacred spirits or divine powers), came into use in order to distinguish indigenous Japanese beliefs from imported Buddhism. While Buddhism is about enlightenment, Shintoism is more about balancing a person's relationship with the spirit world. The kami were thought to be mercurial in demeanor, acting out if displeased and potentially even when appeased, which lead to various shrines, ceremonies, and rituals designed to help humans get along better with the spirits.

Musashi simplified his relationship with the divine, maintaining a respectful reverence yet not counting on otherworldly help. He certainly did not dispute the existence of a god or gods, yet did not expect anything from him/them either. This perspective is pretty much in line with western views of theology as well. For example, the phrase "God helps those who help themselves" is one of the most quoted "biblical" phrases not actually found in the bible. Attributed to Benjamin Franklin (1705 – 1790), it likely originated in ancient Greece. Whatever its origin, this phrase mirrors Musashi's thoughts.

Roman Stoic philosopher Lucius Annaeus Seneca the Younger (4 BC – 65) expressed the same attitude when he wrote, "Luck is when preparation meets opportunity." This, clearly, is what Musashi was getting at. He was always training, always learning, ever prepared to use his unconventional strategy to prevail. A good example of this took place in the year 1612 when he fought a duel against Sasaki Kojirō (1583 – 1612), the preeminent sword master of the time.

Musashi showed up three hours late carrying a wooden *bokken* that he had carved out of an oar rather than a steel *katana*. Since Musashi knew that Kojirō's sword was longer than a normal, he made his wooden sword a bit longer than that too, giving him an advantage in reach. By arriving late, showing contempt for his opponent, and then doubling down by not even having the dignity to use a real sword for a life-or-death duel, he rattled his adversary.

One might think that this would have been enough to prevail, but Musashi was ready to up his advantage given any additional opening. When Kojirō drew his sword, he threw his *saya* (scabbard) aside in disgust... and that is when preparation met opportunity. Musashi unnerved his adversary further by saying, "If you have no more use for your scabbard, you are already dead."

In this fashion Musashi had won before the fight even began. No divine providence, no luck required. He set things up so that he had no option but to prevail in his fight with Kojirō, something he did not once but more than 60 times in duels, and many, many more in skirmishes on the battlefield.

Musashi's position was simple, but yours may be more complex when it comes to your religious or spiritual beliefs. He hedged his bets being courteous when dealing with things divine, yet did not count on them for anything. As you fill out this section of the workbook consider your relationship with the divine. What do you believe? What are your expectations? What do you imagine your responsibilities entail? How does this shape your actions?

What would my world look like if I chose to look at
good luck and bad luck as unavoidable?

Who are my three role models?

1

2

3

What is the one attribute of each of these role models?

1

2

3

What do the three attributes of my role models say
about the key elements of my desires?

1

2

3

What unpleasant thoughts can I face?

Can I own everything instead of blaming luck or God?

When and where have I been using luck or God as an excuse?

Who sows virtue
reaps honor.

Leonardo da Vinci

20.

You May Abandon Your Own Body But You Must Preserve Your HONOR

The idea of preserving one's honor at all costs is difficult to place outside of Japanese culture, especially at the moment in history when Musashi wrote this precept. *Bushido* (way of the warrior), the samurai ethos, is legend. The extremes that many samurai took in preserving their honor were extraordinary.

The story of the 47 *ronin* is a prime example: In 1701 a *daimyo* (territorial lord) named Asano Naganori (1667 – 1701), lord of Ako, traveled to Edo (the capital city) to carry out his duties at the behest of the *shogun* (military ruler) Tokugawa Tsunayoshi (1646 – 1709). Provoked by the arrogance of fellow *daimyo* and master of ceremonies Kira Yoshinaka (1641 – 1703), Asano lost his temper, committing a grave breach of etiquette by drawing his sword and attacking his rival in court. Outraged, the *shogun* ordered Asano to commit *seppuku* (ritual suicide) which he promptly did and was buried at the nearby Sengakuji temple.

Asano's estate was confiscated after his death and his 47 retainers suddenly found themselves *ronin* (masterless samurai). These warriors met in secret, making a pact that their code of honor demanded revenge. They waited a couple of years for Kira to let down his guard, then snuck into his house early one morning in 1703, slaughtering his retainers. They found Kira hiding in an outhouse, cut off his head, and placed it upon their lord's grave completing their vengeance.

While these *ronin* had acted in accordance with *bushido*, they nevertheless flouted the authority of the *shogun,* who ordered them to commit *seppuku*. All of them, ranging in age from fifteen to seventy-seven, promptly obeyed. They were buried in the same temple as Asano and today their graves there have become a visitor attraction. Innumerable poems, essays, and plays have been written about their deeds along with half a dozen movies memorializing their story. In fact, even though the incident took place over three centuries ago, the tale of the 47 *ronin* is considered by many *the* Japanese national legend.

Virtually every culture has some form of honor, especially among the military class. Martial artists and violence professionals tend to be keenly aware of this concept as well. In fact, we are rather fond of the way Teddy Atlas (1956 –), a world-famous boxing trainer and fight commentator phrased it, "You can lose the fight, just do not lose yourself."

Life brings us many choices. Some choices are lateral, others vertical. The lateral choice is about our existing reality, whereas the vertical choice is about our potential, the ascendant reality. The question for you to ponder in the section is how does Musashi's precept enlighten and infuse your life? How does it color your choices on the horizontal and vertical axes?

In what ways do my actions match my mind?

In what ways do my actions match my words?

In what ways do I care about impressing people?

If I do care about impressing people, what
purpose is being served by this act?

List examples where I feel the need to impress even in
the slightest. What does this tell me about myself?

Life is full of duties; some duties have a cost attached.
In what ways am I prepare to pay the fee?

Am I cultivating the virtue(s) that makes
adversity bearable? In what ways?

What can I do to be part of something bigger than myself?

What good can I find inside myself? How can I bring it to the surface?

How well is my spirit dressed?

Is my spirit clear and of purpose? What is my purpose?

How can I make sure none of this goes to my head for good or bad?

Is my attention on the things that hand? In what ways?

As they say in Texas, "Are you all hat and no cattle?"
Do I manifest the trappings but not the
foundation? If so, what can I do about it?

In what ways am I displaying my best qualities?

Where is the path to calmness?

Can I identify the path and then study it to know it? How?

Am I on the path or winging it? In what ways?

I was a bit challenged
when I was younger to
stay on the right path.

Dwayne Johnson

21.

NEVER STRAY FROM THE WAY

The Japanese term *bushido* comes from the root words *bushi,* which means "warrior," and *do,* which denotes a "path" or "way." In other words, it literally translates as "way of the warrior." Akin to a medieval knight's code of chivalry, *bushido* was an ethical system that evangelized certain virtues like courage, honor, loyalty, frugality, and self-control. While the specific qualities promulgated by the *bushido* varied a bit over time, such as before the Genpei War (1180 – 1185), during the Tokugawa shogunate (1603 – 1867), and after the Meiji Restoration (1868 – 1912), they remained thematically consistent over a very long period of time.

In his book *Bushido: The Soul of Japan,* Nitobe Inazō (1862 – 1933) listed the eight virtues of *bushido* as (1) rectitude (justice), (2) courage, (3) benevolence (mercy), (4) politeness, (5) honesty (sincerity), (6) honor, (7) loyalty, and (8) character (self-control). The call to follow this way was so strong in feudal Japan, that any samurai who lost his honor (or believed he was about to) was expected to commit *seppuku,* a particularly painful form of ritual suicide that involved disemboweling oneself before a trusted friend cut off your head (leaving a small flap of skin attached at the front of the neck so that the head would fall forward and not separate from the body).

One can easily imagine *bushido's* influence in Musashi's final precept to stay on the path, to never stray from the way. In our case this means that we must integrate what we have discovered from studying all of the preceding precepts into our daily lives. In other words, we bring our discoveries from Musashi's principles together, internalize them, and place them into application. And, it also means that we must regularly self-audit so that when we find ourselves straying, losing our way, we will be able to realize it, reset, and get ourselves back on course.

So, what is this path? What is your unique, individual way? To be clear, it is not blind adherence to Musashi's precepts, but rather creating your own personal interpretation of what to accept and what to reject from his principles. This must be derived from thoughtful study and analysis of what he wrote. It is everything you have learned so far in building out this workbook, the decisions you have made, and the actions you taken and those you expect to take. These tools can be used in all aspects of your life, and therein lies the greatest power of what the Sword Saint had to say.

Showing up is important, yet it is not a true indicator of whether or not you are actually on the path you have envisioned. Continuous self-audit is necessary, assuring that you have not gone astray. Your unique, individual path forward is informed by your beliefs, background, culture, and values. Consider how your studies may impact your perspective, relationships, and behaviors going forward and whether or not you are actually doing what you told yourself you would do. What is required of you based on what you have determined? How will you fulfil those obligations to yourself?

As you finish this final section, we trust you will have discovered new insight. This book has allowed you to delve into what is true for you. Cutting away those things that no longer belong in your life, rightfully and justly, will bring about the changes you need and desire. As you integrate your new perspective you will gain more power to bolster your direction, more drive to never stray from the way. In this fashion you make the Sword Saint's lessons your own, aligning your heart and mind toward self-improvement.

How can I refresh my mind today in a simple but effective way?

Have I made myself a lifelong project?

If I live today as if it were my last day what would I do?

Are my actions contributing to my well-being? How?

Can I keep life's rhythm no matter the interruption? How?

Where does my lack of self-control create problems?

In what ways is my training designed to help me rise to the occasion?

Am I seeking the beauty of human excellence? How?

Am I staying the course or am I drifting away? How
do I know from moment to moment?

If I took things patiently step-by-step what would I conquer?

Am I on the path to progress? How do I know?

Is it time to stick with it or to quit? What can or should I do differently?

Today's day is _____/_____/_____
Will I seize this day? Yes _____ No _____
What single action will I take this day to seize the day?

Even if you strive diligently
on your chosen path day
after day, if your heart
is not in accord with it,
then even if you think
you are on a good path,
from the point of view of
the straight and true, this
is not a genuine path.

Miyamoto Musashi

CONCLUSION

For the warrior caste in feudal Japan, during Musashi's time, death lurked around every corner. For most of us today, that level of violence is something we have never experienced, nor would we want to, yet there is a certain clarity of meaning that comes from surviving such periods. This perspective is found in Musashi's words, and it is illustrated with the Japanese expression, hakuiki hitotsu ni mo seimei ga yadori, which translates as "life in every breath."

Popularized in the 2003 movie The Last Samurai, this perspective means living in the moment fully, consciously, and intentionally. In such a state, moments linger longer. There is a fullness to even the most mundane experience, say gazing upon a cherry blossom in full bloom, where each and every action we take feels perfectly complete no matter how mundane it may be.

Many of Musashi's precepts center around this concept of living in the moment: accepting everything just the way it is, thinking lightly upon ourselves and deeply on the world, being detached from desire, not regretting what we have done, eschewing jealousy, resentment, and complaint, having no preferences, and not fearing death, to name a few. The connection between mindfulness, living in the moment, and health is both clear and compelling. Mindfulness has been shown to diminish chronic pain, moderate blood pressure, reduce the risk of heart disease, lessen depression, and even slow the progression of certain types of cancer.

Mindfulness is at the root of Buddhism, Taoism, and many Native-American traditions, often applied through meditation or breathing exercises. Life can be stressful enough without compounding it by contemplating everything that can or could go wrong. Negative self-talk had no place in Musashi's world and it should have no influence over ours. When we focus on the life in every breath our tribulations become more manageable, our goals more achievable. In fact, scientific studies demonstrate that mindful people have higher self-esteem even while accepting their own flaws, and as a result are happier, more secure, and more successful.

Now that you have completed the workbook, examine how and where your perspectives on life have changed. Put your thoughts in writing, set them aside, and reflect back upon them a year or two down the road. You will be pleasantly surprised by what you discover.

Thank you!

Thank you for your purchase! Publishing is an arduous process and it is folks like you who make our efforts worthwhile. With roughly 4 million new titles created every year, unbiased customer reviews are indispensable in helping readers identify books that are worth buying. To that end, if you found value from this work, please let other people know. Publish an Amazon review and send us the link at http://www.stickmanpublications.com/contact/ along with your contact information and you will be entered into a drawing to win autographed versions of our four bestselling titles.

About the Authors

Kris Wilder, BCC

Kris was inducted into the US Martial Arts Hall of Fame in 2018. He runs the West Seattle Karate Academy, a frequent destination for practitioners from around the world which also serves the local community. He has earned black belt rankings in three styles, karate, judo, and taekwondo, and often travels to conduct seminars across the United States, Canada, and Europe. His book, The Way of Sanchin Kata, was translated into Japanese, a rare honor for a Western karate practitioner.

A Nationally Board-Certified Life Coach and prolific author, Kris has lectured at Washington State University and Susquehanna University. He spent about 15 years in the political and public affairs arena, working for campaigns from the local to national level. During this consulting career, he was periodically on staff for elected officials. His work also involved lobbying and corporate affairs. And, he was also a member of The Order of St. Francis (OSF), one of many active Apostolic Christian Orders.

Kris is the bestselling author of 22 books, including a Beverly Hills Book Award and Presidential Prize winner, a USA Best Book Awards winner, a National Indie Excellence Awards winner, an Independent Press Award winner, an eLit Book Awards Gold Medal, and a Next Generation Indie Book Awards winner. He has been interviewed on CNN, FOX, The Huffington Post, Thrillist, Nickelodeon, Howard Stern, and more.

Kris lives in Seattle, Washington. You can contact him directly at Kriswilder@kriswilder.com, follow him on Twitter (@kris_wilder), on Facebook (www.facebook.com/kris.wilder) or Instagram (https://www.instagram.com/thekriswilder/).

Lawrence A. Kane, COP-GOV, CSP, CSMP, CIAP

Lawrence was inducted into the Sourcing Industry Group (SIG) Sourcing Supernova Hall of Fame in 2018 for pioneering leadership in strategic sourcing, procurement, supplier innovation, and digital transformation. An Executive Certified Outsourcing Professional, Certified Sourcing Professional, Certified Supplier Management Professional, and Certified Intelligent Automation Professional, he currently works as a senior leader at a Fortune® 50 corporation where he gets to play with billions of dollars of other people's money and make really important decisions.

A martial artist, judicious use-of-force expert, and the bestselling author of 20 books, he has won numerous awards including the 2021 Independent Press Award, the 5th Annual Beverly Hills Book Award and Presidential Prize, the 13th Annual USA Best Book Awards winner, the 11th and 14th Annual National Indie Excellence Awards winner, a Next Generation Indie Book Awards winner, an eLit Book Awards Gold Medal, 3 ForeWord Magazine Book of the Year Award finalists, 5 USA Book News Best Books Award finalists, 3 Next Generation Indie Book Awards finalists, 2 Beverly Hills Book Awards finalists, and an eLit Book Awards Bronze prize.

Since 1970, Lawrence has studied and taught traditional Asian martial arts, medieval European combat, and modern close-quarter weapon techniques. Working stadium security part-time for 26 years he was involved in hundreds of violent altercations, but got paid to watch football. A founding technical consultant to University of New Mexico's Institute of Traditional Martial Arts, he has also written hundreds of articles on martial arts, self-defense, countervailing force, and related topics.

He has been interviewed numerous times on podcasts (e.g., Art of Procurement, Negotiations Ninja Podcast), nationally syndicated and local radio shows (e.g., Biz Talk Radio, The Jim Bohannon Show), and television programs (e.g., Fox Morning News) as well as by reporters from Computerworld, Le Matin, Practical Taekwondo, Forbes, Traditional Karate, and Police Magazine, among other publications. He was once interviewed in English by a reporter from a Swiss newspaper for an article that was published in French, and found that oddly amusing.

Lawrence lives in Seattle, Washington. You can contact him directly at lakane@ix.netcom.com or connect with him on LinkedIn (www.linkedin.com/in/lawrenceakane).

Non-Fiction Books

Musashi's Dokkodo (Kane/Wilder)

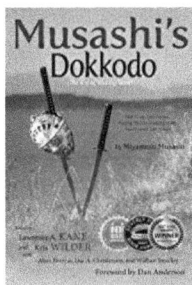

"The authors have made classic samurai wisdom accessible to the modern martial artist like never before" – **Goran Powell**, award winning author of *Chojun* and *A Sudden Dawn*

Shortly before he died, Miyamoto Musashi (1584 – 1645) wrote down his final thoughts about life for his favorite student Terao Magonojō to whom Go Rin No Sho, his famous Book of Five Rings, had also been dedicated. He called this treatise Dokkodo, which translates as "The Way of Walking Alone." This treatise contains Musashi's original 21 precepts of the Dokkodo along with five different interpretations of each passage written from the viewpoints of a monk, a warrior, a teacher, an insurance executive, and a businessman. In this fashion you are not just reading a simple translation of Musashi's writing, you are scrutinizing his final words for deeper meaning. In them are enduring lessons for how to lead a successful and meaningful life.

10 Rules of Karate (Wilder/Kane)

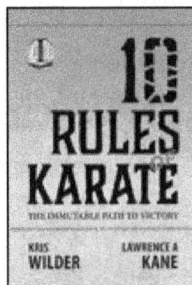

"Since losing is not an option on or off the mat, this is an absolute must read for karateka." – **Christian Wedewardt**, Founder & Head of Karatepraxis

All ten precepts in this concise book cut to the heart of ending physical confrontations as quickly as possible with empty-hand techniques. Our definition of "ending" is to make the attack stop. There is no running after the now fleeing assailant to catch and strike him down. There is no lesson, no teaching, no therapy, no epiphany. There is only making that bad guy stop what he is doing instantly so that you and those you care about will be safe. These principles are style agnostic, all about ending fights immediately. They define how to best apply your skills and training in the real world. Those who work with these principles will find swiftness, clarity, and victory in so doing.

The Little Black Book of Violence (Kane/Wilder)

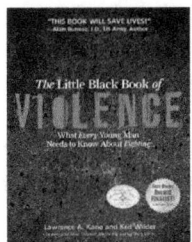

"This book will save lives!" – **Alain Burrese**, JD, former US Army 2nd Infantry Division Scout Sniper School instructor

Men commit 80% of all violent crimes and are twice as likely to become the victims of aggressive behavior. This book is primarily written for men ages 15 to 35, and contains more than mere self-defense techniques. You will learn crucial information about street survival that most martial arts instructors don't even know. Discover how to use awareness, avoidance, and de—escalation to help stave off violence, know when it's prudent to fight, and understand how to do so effectively when fighting is unavoidable.

Sh!t Sun Tzu Said (Kane/Wilder)

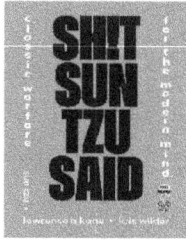

"If you had to choose one variant of Sun Tzu's collected work, this one should be at the top of the pile... I loved it!" – **Jeffrey-Peter Hauck**, MSc, JD, Police SGT (Ret.), LPI, CPT USA, Professor of Criminal Justice

Sun Tzu was a famous Chinese general whose mastery of strategy was so exceptional that he reportedly transformed 180 courtesans into skilled soldiers in a single training session. While that episode was likely exaggerated, historians agree that Sun Tzu defeated the Ch'u, Qi, and Chin states for King Ho-Lu, forging his empire. In 510 BC, Master Tzu recorded his winning strategies in Art of War, the earliest surviving and most revered tome of its kind. With methods so powerful they can conquer an adversary's spirit, you can use Master Tzu's strategies to overcome any challenge, from warfare to self-defense to business negotiations. This book starts with the classic 1910 translation of Art of War, adds modern and historical insight, and demonstrates how to put the master's timeless wisdom to use in your everyday life. In this fashion, the Art of War becomes accessible for the modern mind, simultaneously entertaining, enlightening, and practical.

The Big Bloody Book of Violence (Kane/Wilder)

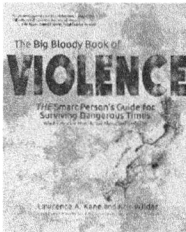

"Implementing even a fraction of this book's suggestions will substantially increase your overall safety." – **Gila Hayes**, Armed Citizens' Legal Defense Network

All throughout history ordinary people have been at risk of violence in one way or another. Abdicating personal responsibility by outsourcing your safety to others might be the easy way out, but it does little to safeguard your welfare. In this book you'll discover what dangers you face and learn proven strategies to thwart them. Self-defense is far more than fighting skills; it's a lifestyle choice, a more enlightened way of looking at and moving through the world. Learn to make sense of "senseless" violence, overcome talisman thinking, escape riots, avert terrorism, circumvent gangs, defend against home invasions, safely interact with law enforcement, and conquer seemingly impossible odds.

Dude, The World's Gonna Punch You in the Face (Wilder/Kane)

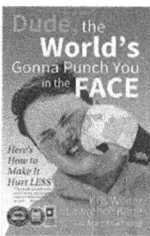

"As an emergency room physician, I see a lot of injuries. This book can save you a lot of pain and trauma, not just physical but also emotional and financial as well. Do yourself a favor, read it, and stay out of my Emergency Room." – **Jeff Cooper**, MD

We only get one shot at life. And, it's really easy to screw that up because the world wants to punch us all in the face. Hard! But, what if you knew when to duck? What if you were warned about the dangers—and possibilities—ahead of time? Here is how to man-up and take on whatever the world throws at you. This powerful book arms young men with knowledge about love, wealth, education, faith, government, leadership, work, relationships, life, and violence. It won't prevent all mistakes, nothing will, but it can keep you from making the impactful ones that you'll regret the most. This book is quick knowledge, easy to read, and brutally frank, just the way the world gives it to you, except without the pain. Read on. Learn how to see the bad things coming and avoid them.

Sensei Mentor Teacher Coach (Wilder/Kane)

"Finally, a book that will actually move the needle in closing the leadership skills gap found in all aspects of our society." – **Dan Roberts**, CEO and President, Ouellette & Associates

Many books weave platitudes, promising the keys to success in leadership, secrets that will transform you into the great leader, the one. The fact of the matter is, however, that true leadership really isn't about you. It's about giving back, offering your best to others so that they can find the best in themselves.

The methodologies in this book help you become the leader you were meant to be by bringing your goals and other peoples' needs together to create a powerful, combined vision. Learn how to access the deeper aspects of who you are, your unique qualities, and push them forward in actionable ways. Acquire this vital information and advance your leadership journey today.

Dirty Ground (Kane/Wilder)

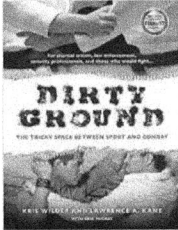

"Fills a void in martial arts training." – **Loren W. Christensen**, Martial Arts Masters Hall of Fame member

This book addresses a significant gap in most martial arts training, the tricky space that lies between sport and combat applications where you need to control a person without injuring him (or her). Techniques in this region are called "drunkle," named after the drunken uncle disrupting a family gathering. Understanding how to deal with combat, sport, and drunkle situations is vital because appropriate use of force is codified in law and actions that do not accommodate these regulations can have severe repercussions. Martial arts techniques must be adapted to best fit the situation you find yourself in. This book shows you how.

Scaling Force (Kane/Miller)

"If you're serious about learning how the application of physical force works—before, during and after the fact—I cannot recommend this book highly enough." – **Lt. Jon Lupo**, New York State Police

Conflict and violence cover a broad range of behaviors, from intimidation to murder, and require an equally broad range of responses. A kind word will not resolve all situations, nor will wristlocks, punches, or even a gun. This book introduces the full range of options, from skillfully doing nothing to employing deadly force. You will understand the limits of each type of force, when specific levels may be appropriate, the circumstances under which you may have to apply them, and the potential costs, legally and personally, of your decision. If you do not know how to succeed at all six levels covered in this book there are situations in which you will have no appropriate options. More often than not, that will end badly.

Surviving Armed Assaults (Kane)

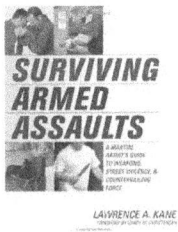

"This book will be an invaluable resource for anyone walking the warrior's path, and anyone who is interested in this vital topic." – **Lt. Col. Dave Grossman**, Director, Warrior Science Group

A sad fact is that weapon-wielding thugs victimize 1,773,000 citizens every year in the United States alone. Even martial artists are not immune from this deadly threat. Consequently, self-defense training that does not consider the very real possibility of an armed attack is dangerously incomplete. You should be both mentally and physically prepared to deal with an unprovoked armed assault at any time. Preparation must be comprehensive enough to account for the plethora of pointy objects, blunt instruments, explosive devices, and deadly projectiles that someday could be used against you. This extensive book teaches proven survival skills that can keep you safe.

The 87—Fold Path to Being the Best Martial Artist (Kane/Wilder)

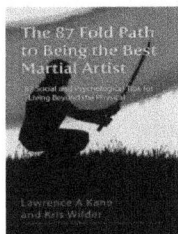

"The 87—Fold Path contains unexpected, concise blows to the head and heart... you don't have a chance, but to examine and retool your way of life." – **George Rohrer**, Executive and Purpose Coach, MBA, CPCC, PCC

Despite the fact that raw materials in feudal Japan were mediocre at best, bladesmiths used innovative techniques to forge some of the finest swords imaginable for their samurai overlords. The process of heating and folding the metal removed impurities, while shaping and strengthening the blades to perfection. The end result was strong yet supple, beautiful and deadly. As martial artists we utilize a similar process, forging our bodies through hard work, perseverance, and repetition. Knowing how to fight is important, clearly, yet if you do not find something larger than base violence attached your efforts it becomes unsustainable. *The 87-Fold Path* provides ideas for taking your training beyond the physical that are uniquely tailored for the elite martial artist.

How to Win a Fight (Kane/Wilder)

"It is the ultimate course in self-defense and will help you survive and get through just about any violent situation or attack." – **Jeff Rivera**, bestselling author

More than 3,000,000 Americans are involved in a violent physical encounter every year. Develop the fortitude to walk away when you can and prevail when you must. Defense begins by scanning your environment, recognizing hazards and escape routes, and using verbal de-escalation to defuse tense situations. If a fight is unavoidable, the authors offer clear guidance for being the victor, along with advice on legal implications, including how to handle a police interview after the altercation.

Lessons from the Dojo Floor (Wilder)

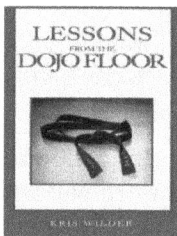

"Helps each reader, from white belt to black belt, look at and understand why he or she trains." – **Michael E. Odell**, *Isshin-Ryu* Northwest Okinawa Karate Association

In the vein of Dave Lowry, a thought-provoking collection of short vignettes that entertains while it educates. Packed with straightforward, easy, and quick to read sections that range from profound to insightful to just plain amusing, anyone with an affinity for martial arts can benefit from this material. This book educates, entertains, and ultimately challenges every martial artist from beginner to black belt.

Martial Arts Instruction (Kane)

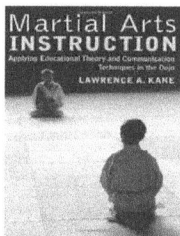

"Boeing trains hundreds of security officers, Kane's ideas will help us be more effective." – **Gregory A. Gwash**, Chief Security Officer, The Boeing Company

While the old adage, "those who can't do, teach," is not entirely true, all too often "those who can do" cannot teach effectively. This book is unique in that it offers a holistic approach to teaching martial arts; incorporating elements of educational theory and communication techniques typically overlooked in *budo* (warrior arts). Teachers will improve their abilities to motivate, educate, and retain students, while students interested in the martial arts will develop a better understanding of what instructional method best suits their needs.

The Way of Kata (Kane/Wilder)

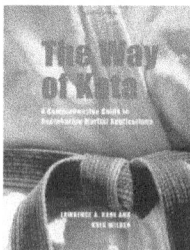

"This superb book is essential reading for all those who wish to understand the highly effective techniques, concepts, and strategies that the kata were created to record." – **Iain Abernethy**, British Combat Association Hall of Fame member

The ancient masters developed *kata*, or "formal exercises," as fault—tolerant methods to preserve their unique, combat-proven fighting systems. Unfortunately, they also deployed a two-track system of instruction where only the select inner circle that had gained a master's trust and respect would be taught the powerful hidden applications of *kata*. The theory of deciphering *kata* was once a great mystery revealed only to trusted disciples of the ancient masters in order to protect the secrets of their systems. Even today, while the basic movements of *kata* are widely known, the principles and rules for understanding *kata* applications are largely unknown. This groundbreaking book unveils these methods, not only teaching you how to analyze your *kata* to understand what it is trying to tell you, but also helping you to utilize your fighting techniques more effectively.

The Way of Martial Arts for Kids (Wilder)

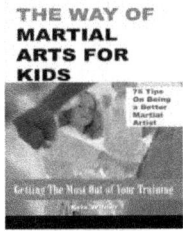

"Written in a personable, engaging style that will appeal to kids and adults alike." – **Laura Weller**, Guitarist, The Green Pajamas

Based on centuries of traditions, martial arts training can be a positive experience for kids. The book helps you and yours get the most out of every class. It shows how just about any child can become one of those few exemplary learners who excel in the training hall as well as in life. Written to children, it is also for parents as well. After all, while the martial arts instructor knows his art, no one knows his/her child better than the parent. Together you can help your child achieve just about anything... The advice provided is straightforward, easy to understand, and written with a child-reader in mind so that it can either be studied by the child and/or read together with the parent to assure solid results.

The Way of Sanchin Kata (Wilder)

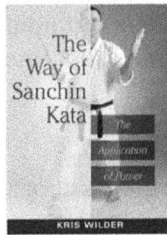

"This book has been sorely needed for generations!" – **Philip Starr**, National Chairman, Yiliquan Martial Arts Association

When karate was first developed in Okinawa it was about using technique and extraordinary power to end a fight instantly. These old ways of generating remarkable power are still accessible, but they are purposefully hidden in *sanchin kata* for the truly dedicated to find. This book takes the practitioner to new depths of practice by breaking down the form piece-by-piece, body part by body part, so that the very foundation of the *kata* is revealed. Every chapter, concept, and application is accompanied by a "Test It" section, designed for you to explore and verify the *kata* for yourself. *Sanchin kata* really comes alive when you feel the thrill of having those hidden teachings speak to you across the ages through your body. Simply put, once you read this book and test what you have learned, your karate will never be the same.

Journey: The Martial Artist's Notebook (Kane/Wilder)

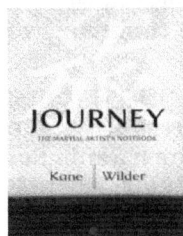

"Students who take notes progress faster and enjoy a deeper understanding than those who don't. Period." – **Loren W. Christensen**, Martial Arts Masters Hall of Fame inductee

As martial arts students progress through the lower ranks it is extraordinarily useful for them to keep a record of what they have learned. The mere process of writing things down facilitates deeper understanding. This concept is so successful, in fact, that many schools require advanced students to complete a thesis or research project concurrent with testing for black belt rank, advancing the knowledge base of the organization while simultaneously clarifying and adding depth to each practitioner's understanding of his or her art. Just as Bruce Lee's notes and essays became *Tao of Jeet Kune Do*, perhaps someday your training journal will be published for the masses, but first and foremost this notebook is by you, for you. This is where the deeper journey on your martial path toward mastery begins.

The Way to Black Belt (Kane/Wilder)

"It is so good I wish I had written it myself." – **Hanshi Patrick McCarthy**, Director, International *Ryukyu* Karate Research Society

Cut to the very core of what it means to be successful in the martial arts. Earning a black belt can be the most rewarding experience of a lifetime, but getting there takes considerable planning. Whether your interests are in the classical styles of Asia or in today's Mixed Martial Arts (MMA), this book prepares you to meet every challenge. Whatever your age, whatever your gender, you will benefit from the wisdom of master martial artists around the globe, including Iain Abernethy, Dan Anderson,

Loren Christensen, Jeff Cooper, Wim Demeere, Aaron Fields, Rory Miller, Martina Sprague, Phillip Starr, and many more, who share more than 300 years of combined training experience. Benefit from their guidance during your development into a first-class black belt.

Wolves in Street Clothing (Wilder/ Hollingsworth)

"Teaches folks to rekindle tools that are already in us—already in our DNA—and have been there for thousands of years." – **Ron Jarvis**, Tracker, Outdoorsman, Self-Defense Instructor

This book gives you a new light in which to see human predatory behavior. As we move farther and farther from our roots insulating ourselves in technology and air-conditioned homes we get disconnected from the inherent and innate aspects of understanding the precursors to violent behavior. Violence is not always emotionally bound, often and in the animal kingdom is simply a tool to access a needed resource—or to protect an essential resource. Distance, encroachment, and signals are keys to avoiding a predator. Why would a cougar attack a man after a bike ride? Why would a bear attack a man in a hot tub? Why would a thug rob one person and not another? The predatory animal mind holds many of the keys to the answer to these questions. Learn drills that will help you tune your focus and move through life safer and more aware of your surroundings.

70-Second Sensei (Kane/Wilder)

"I'll let you in on a secret. The 70-Second Sensei is a gateway drug. It's short, easy to read, and useful. It has stuff in it that will make you a better instructor. Even a better person." — **Rory Miller**, Chiron Training

Once you have mastered the physical aspects of your martial art, it is time to take it to the next level—to lead, to teach, to leave a legacy. This innovative book shows you how. Sensei is a Japanese word, commonly translated as "teacher," which literally means "one who has come before." This term is usually applied to martial arts instructors, yet it can signify anyone who has blazed a trail for others to follow. It applies to all those who have acquired valuable knowledge, skills, and experience and are willing to share their expertise with others while continuing to grow themselves. After all, setting an example that others wish to emulate is the very essence of leadership. Clearly you cannot magically become an exemplary martial arts instructor in a mere 70-seconds any more than a businessperson can transform his or her leadership style from spending 60-seconds perusing The One Minute Manager. You can, however, devote a few minutes a day to honing your craft. It is about giving back, offering your best to others so that they can find the best in themselves. And, with appreciation, they can pay it forward...

The Contract Professional's Playbook (Nyden/Kane)

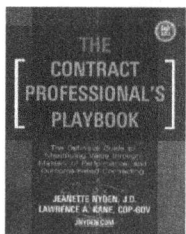

"While early career practitioners may understand the value of drafting, negotiating, and managing exceptional contracts, they often struggle to master the requisite skills. This comprehensive manual helps structure the negotiation process, thereby minimizing the perilous process of trial-and-error, expediting competency with leading practices and tools that can help reduce risk and speed outcomes for both buy-side and sell-side alike." — **Gregg Kirchhoefer**, P.C., IAOP Leadership Hall of Fame Member

Ever increasing demand for performance- and outcome-based agreements stems from pressure for enterprises to drive greater value from their strategic customer/supplier relationships. To achieve expected performance, contractual relationships are increasingly complex and interdependent, requiring more stakeholders be involved in the decision making. Unfortunately for contract professionals held accountable to these requirements there has been little in the way of resources that answer their "how to" questions about drafting, negotiating, and managing performance- and outcome-based agreements. Until now! *The Contract Professional's Playbook* (and corresponding eLearning program) walks subject matter experts who may be new to complex contracting step-by-step through all aspects of the contract life cycle. Invaluable competencies include identifying and managing risk, increasing influence with stakeholders, developing pricing models, negotiating complex deals, and governing customer-supplier relationships to avoid value leakage in the midst of constant change. It's an invaluable resource that raises the bar for buy-side and sell-side practitioners alike.

<u>There are Angels in My Head!</u> (Wilder)

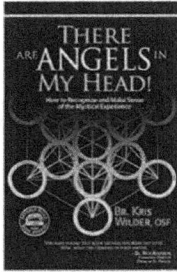

"This is not a book on doctrine, dogma or collection of creeds to memorize in order to impress others with knowledge. This is a practical application of your participation in a new experience. Here you will find your questions answered even before they are asked." – **Br. Rich Atkinson**, Order of St. Francis

The unexplainable has happened. A prayer has been answered, a gift has been given, a communication has occurred... Is it the voice of God, or the voices in your head? Here's how to find out: In this groundbreaking book, you will discover the organization of the mystical experience. Based on the classic works of G. B Scaramelli, an 18th Century Jesuit Priest, Wilder brings modern relevance to any person to apply to their journey as they seek the Divine. Using examples and principles from Christianity and other religions, Wilder demonstrates that mankind's profound mystical experience crosses all cultures and religions.

Fiction Books

Blinded by the Night (Kane)

"Kane's expertise in matters of mayhem shines throughout." – **Steve Perry**, bestselling author

Richard Hayes is a Seattle cop. After 25 years on the force he thinks he knows everything there is to know about predators. Rapists, murderers, gang bangers, and child molesters are just another day at the office, yet commonplace criminals become the least of his problems when he goes hunting for a serial killer and runs into a real monster. The creature not only attacks him, but merely gets pissed off when he shoots it. In the head. Twice! Surviving that fight is only the beginning. Richard discovers that the vampire he destroyed was the ruler of an eldritch realm he never dreamed existed. By some archaic rule, having defeated the monster's sovereign in battle, Richard becomes their new king. When it comes to human predators, Richard is a seasoned veteran, yet with paranormal ones he is but a rookie. He must navigate a web of intrigue and survive long enough to discover how a regular guy can tangle with supernatural creatures and prevail.

Legends of the Masters (Kane/Wilder)

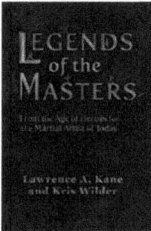

"It is a series of (very) short stories teaching life lessons. I'm going to bring it out when my nephews are over at family dinners for good discussion starters. A fun read!" – **Angela Palmore**

Storytelling is an ancient form of communication that still resonates today. An engaging story told and retold shares a meaningful message that can be passed down through the generations. Take fables such as *The Boy Who Cried Wolf* or *The Tortoise and the Hare*, who hasn't learned a thing or two from these ancient tales? This book retools Aesop's lesser-known fables, reimagining them to meet the needs and interests of modern martial artists. Reflecting upon the wisdom of yesteryear in this new light will surely bring value for practitioners of the arts today.

DVDs

121 Killer Appz (Wilder/Kane)

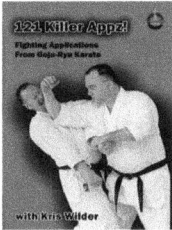

"Quick and brutal, the way karate is meant to be." – **Eric Parsons**, Founder, Karate for Life Foundation

You know the *kata*, now it is time for the applications. *Gekisai (dai ni), Saifa, Seiyunchin, Seipai, Kururunfa, Suparinpei, Sanseiru, Shisochin,* and *Seisan kata* are covered. If you ever wondered what purpose a move from a *Goju Ryu* karate form was for, wonder no longer. This DVD contains no discussion, just a no-nonsense approach to one application after another. It illuminates your *kata* and stimulates deeper thought on determining your own applications from the *Goju Ryu* karate forms.

Sanchin Kata: Three Battles Karate Kata (Wilder)

"A cornucopia of martial arts knowledge." – **Shawn Kovacich**, endurance high—kicking world record holder (as certified by the Guinness Book of World Records)

A traditional training method for building karate power, *sanchin kata* is an ancient form. Some consider it the missing link between Chinese kung fu and Okinawan karate. This program breaks down the form piece by piece, body part by body part, so that the hidden details of the *kata* are revealed. This DVD complements the book *The Way of Sanchin Kata*, providing in-depth exploration of the form, with detailed instruction of the essential posture, linking the spine, generating power, and demonstration of the complete *kata*.

Scaling Force (Miller/Kane)

"Kane and Miller have been there, done that and have the t—shirt. And they're giving you their lessons learned without requiring you to pay the fee in blood they had to in order to learn them. That is priceless." – **M. Guthrie**, Federal Air Marshal

Conflict and violence cover a broad range of behaviors, from intimidation to murder, and they require an equally broad range of responses. A kind word will not resolve all situations, nor will wristlocks, punches, or even a gun. Miller and Kane explain and demonstrate the full range of options, from skillfully doing nothing to applying deadly force. You will learn to understand the limits of each type of force, when specific levels may be appropriate, the circumstances under which you may have to apply them, and the potential cost of your decision, legally and personally. If you do not know how to succeed at all six levels, there are situations in which you will have no appropriate options. That tends to end badly. This DVD complements the book *Scaling Force*.

Accept everything just the way it is

Do not seek pleasure for its own sake

Do not under any circumstances depend on a partial feeling

Think lightly of yourself and deeply of the world

Be detached from desire your whole life long

Do not regret what you have done

Never be jealous

Never let yourself be saddened by separation

Resentment and complaint are appropriate neither for oneself nor others

Do not let yourself be guided by the feelings of lust or love

Have no preferences in all things

Be indifferent to where you live

Do not pursue the taste of good food

Do not hold onto what you no longer need

Do not act following customary beliefs

Do not collect weapons or practice with weapons beyond what is useful

Do not fear death

Do not seek to possess either goods or fiefs for your old age

Respect Buddha and the gods without counting on their help

You may abandon your own body but you must preserve your honor

Never stray from the way

www.ingramcontent.com/pod-product-compliance
Lightning Source LLC
Chambersburg PA
CBHW080605090426
42735CB00017B/3342